The Navigator

The Navigator

BY ROBERT D. FOSTER

CHALLENGE BOOKS, Ltd

BOX 1118
COLORADO SPRINGS
COLORADO 80901

© 1983 by Robert D. Foster
All rights reserved, including translation
Library of Congress Catalog Card Number:
  83-060287
ISBN: 0-89109-495-4
14951

Fifth Printing, 1991

Scripture quotations are from the *King James Version* unless otherwise noted. Other versions used are *The Amplified New Testament (AMP)*, © 1954, 1958 by The Lockman Foundation; *The Living Bible (LB)*, © 1971 by Tyndale House Publishers, Wheaton, Illinois, and used by permission; the *Holy Bible: New Internationl Version* (NIV), © 1978 by the International Bible Society, used by permission of Zondervan Bible Publishers; and *The New Testament in Modern English (Phillips)*, © 1958, 1972 by J. B. Phillips.

Printed in the United States of America

To Lorne Sanny

a stalwart buddy
in the cause of Christ

a sharer
in the disciplines of Godliness

a shining example
of "a little one becoming a thousand"

a soldier of the Cross
who has lived solely for the glory of God
and the spread of the Gospel

this volume is affectionately dedicated.

Contents

Foreword

Dawson Trotman was one of the most unforgettable characters I have ever met in Christian work. He was always helping someone wherever he went. He was on duty at all times, touching lives daily—and sometimes hourly—for Christ. In his excellent book entitled *The Navigator*, my longtime friend Bob Foster (whose life is also thrilling and should be written about sometime) has explored how and why God used this unique and dedicated man, so that you too will become more committed to Jesus Christ.

When I was a student pastor in Wheaton, Illinois, I had heard much about the organization called The Navigators, founded by Dawson Trotman. I asked Dawson if he would preach for me one Sunday. He did, and he made a tremendous impact—not only on my congregation, but on the college as well.

From that moment on he became one of my best friends and advisors.

During our Los Angeles Crusade of 1949, which was the first Crusade that received national attention, we asked Dawson to help us in counseling and follow-up. In those days we called people "personal workers," and we had a minimum of follow-up. It had always been Cliff Barrows's and my custom to go into an adjoining tent and speak to and pray with each individual personally. We had kept that up for several years.

When Dawson Trotman joined our efforts, he began to develop follow-up literature for us and to make suggestions from time to time about the best way to accomplish this important task. (In the meantime, Daws was training Lorne Sanny. More and more he turned the counseling and follow-up of our Crusades over to Lorne.) The very extensive follow-up system we now have, which I think is the most intensive and extensive in the history of so-called "mass evangelism," actually came from Dawson Trotman's heart and mind.

At the same time that he was helping us with Crusade follow-up, as you will read in Bob Foster's account, Daws was developing The Navigators into some of the most highly skilled people in the use of Scripture, soul-winning, and discipleship to be found in the Christian world. He left thousands with principles of Christian growth to live by.

As Bob Foster shows in this book, Daws was unconventional—a man's man, rough and tough at times. Though he was a tenacious person, he was kind and understanding. He was serious but had a sense of humor, and at times was even a practical joker.

Daws was a born optimist with a strong faith. He knew how to motivate people and get them to work. He spent much time in prayer with those he contacted. I can remember even in Switzerland, in the earlier days of our evangelism, going out and having long prayer meetings with him. He would come to my hotel room, or I would go to his room, and we would kneel down and cry out to the Lord.

The mechanical wheel that Daws designed to get his primary message across in effect became his logo. Christ was at the hub or center of the wheel, then on the spokes were The Word, Prayer, Obedience, and Witnessing. Dawson was known for his devotion to the Scriptures, and he constantly challenged every believer to memorize God's Word, emphasizing repetition as the best way to retain it. He was deeply dedicated to evangelism and follow-up.

Dawson Trotman was a man I shall never forget—"always about his Father's business."

BILLY GRAHAM

Preface

This book concerns more than just what the Lord
enabled his servant, Dawson Trotman, to do over a
short lifespan of fifty years. It is an attempt to glean
from his messages and personal aquaintances what
he believed and taught, and why. What was his
unique contribution to the church? Why do the
words, "The foundations of many generations"
apply particularly to him?

It is the search for answers to these questions

that has spurred me on to understand the nature of this man of God. There are usually four ways to gain such an understanding: Search his words to uncover his ideas and thoughts; look closely at his character and convictions to understand his motivation; study the institutions he may have left behind; and finally, look at the lives of the men he discipled and motivated to carry out his vision. (For a comprehensive and chronological treatment of Dawson Trotman's life, I recommend Betty Skinner's excellent biography, *Daws*, published by Zondervan, 1974.)

Dawson did not do much writing. He was too busy making disciples. His monument was left not in marble, but in men; not in books, but in methods for living by scriptural truth; not in institutions, but in principles for multiplying Christian disciples around the world.

Introduction

On the afternoon of June 18, 1956, a speedboat skimmed across the cold waters of Schroon Lake in upstate New York. Suddenly a wave struck the boat, hurling two of its occupants into the water. The man held the young girl's head above the water until she was rescued—then he suddenly sank and disappeared.

Time magazine told the world about his death in its religion section for July 2, 1956. Under his picture was this caption: "Always Holding Someone Up." The article began, "So died Dawson Trotman, 'The Navigator,' light and power of a movement that echoes the Words of the Scriptures around the world."

Who was Dawson Trotman, and why did his death receive mention in the secular press?

Many Christian leaders now recognize that in his thirty years of service for God, Daws had been used to help bring back into focus for the Christian world some foundational Bible truths which had been forgotten for years—the importance of personal follow-up of new Christian converts, the one-on-one training of disciples, and the multiplication of disciples as a means of carrying out the Great Commission.

What Orville and Wilbur Wright were to commercial flight, Dawson was to discipleship in the church. He had a basic vision. Although his applications were refined by others, he was a pioneer—one who makes things happen.

Evangelist Billy Graham said of him in 1956, "I think Dawson touched more lives than any man I have ever known. We today are only representatives of thousands of many races and languages and cultures that have been influenced by this great man. . . ."

In reviewing the legacy of Dawson Trotman, Lorne Sanny, successor to Dawson as president of

The Navigators, said, "Dawson did not primarily leave a lifework complete with fruit that would remain—although he did that! Nor did he leave spiritual methods which could be set in motion and left to continue by themselves—although he did that! Rather, Daws left a life principle embodied in men who have found in it their own fruitfulness and vision—the vision of multiplication of disciples by a person-to-person method, with each person so reached becoming a soulwinner and teacher of others, who would be a reacher and teacher of others. Thousands of lives have now been touched, not through the magic of a personality nor the cleverness of methods, but by a man determined to find what God wanted and to trust Him for methods to carry it out, all the time believing God's Word."

Cameron Townsend, the late founder of Wycliffe Bible Translators and one of Dawson's closest partners, described Dawson by relating this humorous incident: "One time while in Los Angeles on a short speaking tour, I was suffering from a severe pain in my back. It was difficult to move, let alone carry out my speaking responsibilities.

"Somehow I finally got through the weekend. As Bill Nyman was taking me to the railway station in Pasadena, we stopped by the Navigator office in Eagle Rock so that I could tell Daws goodbye, even though I didn't feel like getting out of the car because of the pain.

"Slowly we walked into his office. 'Cam, what's the problem? You're walking like an old man!' Dawson grabbed me, gave me a powerful bear hug, and guess what? Something snapped in my back as he did this and the pain was gone! Daws always did things with zest! But this was his lifestyle . . . going around the world, moving among Christian organizations and church people, giving them powerful bear hugs which often removed the pain and hurt that they had been suffering."

It was this vitality and drive that the veteran missionary leader, Hubert Mitchell, expressed so clearly: "Daws was a rough hewn, hard-hitting Christian. He was a man's man, and that's what drew me to him. He was so powerful in that he was always preaching on that which he lived and believed in and was willing to lay his life on the line for. Dawson never formally studied much church history, theology, and Greek and Hebrew, but his practical experience with God was real, and God used him for these reasons."

The secret of his life was that he had a gargantuan bent toward God, and he was tenacious in his quest to know Christ. This determination and tenacity was evident in his early achievement in hiding God's Word in his heart: "I learned my first one thousand Bible verses by just having a goal to learn one a day . . . every day for one thousand days. I'd never have done it if I hadn't pushed for that old one hundred percent record. The same applies to witnessing for Christ. The early Minutemen of our work had a goal to touch one life a day, learn one verse a day, and spend one hour a day with God in personal devotions. I'd rather do anything than have to check that I had failed. It's human nature to be lazy. But the Lord knows that, and so He has given us a brain to figure out how to overcome any obstacle that the enemy puts in our way to keep us from carrying out His orders."

"Carrying out His orders" was the thrust of Dawson Trotman, a servant of God.

1906	March 25, Dawson Earle Trotman, born in Bisbee, Arizona.
1926	Began his spiritual odyssey with God in Lomita, California.
1932	Married his teenage sweetheart, Lila Clayton.
1934	Navigator name officially placed on the ministry with the motto: "To know Christ and to make Him known."
1956	June 18, Dawson drowned in Schroon Lake, New York.

Behold, I will do a new thing;
now it shall spring forth; shall
ye not know it? I will even
make a way in the wilderness,
and rivers in the desert.

ISAIAH 43:19

Chapter 1

New Wine

The years of Dawson's life, 1906 to 1956, were a phenomenal half century—fifty years of enormous achievement with breathtaking velocity.

At the heart of this time period the United States sat depressed, bewildered, and unsure of its role and purpose in world affairs. Then, on December 7, 1941, America broke forth angrily to become, four years later, one of the victors in a great worldwide war. Later, having learned from the disciplines of both the Great Depression and World War II, the Western world, including America, began a process of sowing the seeds of two great humanitarian concepts: liberty and abundance. Western governments believed that no impoverished person could be really free, and that no man in a free society need be impoverished.

At the very time that Dawson Trotman and Lila Clayton were exchanging their marriage vows in the South Lomita Bible Church in 1932, there was disillusionment and discouragement in the United States. A once optimistic people in the 1920s, Americans now seemed resigned to the inevitability of history's cycle.

National upheaval

There were three factors that weighed heavily upon the citizens of the United States during the 1930s and 1940s. First, the Wall Street financial collapse of 1929 brought about a political and economic crisis in American life that left this nation in a deep depression. Second, the war machines of Germany and Japan were cranking up to bring worldwide political unrest as U.S. President Franklin D. Roosevelt was trying to lead the nation out of the great depression. New models of labor organization, governmental agencies, and military preparedness were proposed and implemented in his famous "New Deal," which some applauded, yet others denounced.

Finally, there was a theological upheaval. The mainline denominations of that period were deeply institutionalized in their mission. The fundamentalists, those who insisted on a return to orthodoxy and the "fundamentals" of Christianity, began taking the offensive in church planting, youth work, and foreign missions. The "modernists" were considered the enemy of the gospel. The Eighteenth Amendment to the Constitution created Prohibition —days of negativism to liquor and booze, but also days of apathy and indifference to spiritual needs here at home and abroad by the institutional church.

But underneath the apathy of the "establishment," God was at work in new ways. The old wine skins of the church couldn't hold the spiritual ferment, and so new ministries and outreaches began. This was the heyday of the Bible School movement, the Independent Foreign Mission Societies, Independent Seminaries, and the Independent Bible churches. Almost every thrust went independent. Because of the loss of jobs, lack of food, and liquidation of social structures, the "skid rows" of our major cities were burgeoning, and with that growth came the great Union Rescue Mission movement to reach these "down-and-outers."

"Separation" was the spirit of the decade up and down the church structure. Bogged down with the sheer weight of its theological and ecclesiastical confusion, the Protestant vehicle blew a tire.

The great American cultural jalopy needed a pit stop. The financial crisis, the political unrest, and the theological upheaval left us out of gas, flat-tired, and in need of an overhaul.

Spiritual stirrings

But out of all this came stirrings of hope. New wine of the Holy Spirit's fermenting became available, money problems caused people to reevaluate their basic values, and World War II became a crusade, something to give your life to—which many of our young men literally did on battlefields around the world.

The twenty-year period from 1926 to 1946 might have looked like a disaster for the church, but God was secretly at work. These were the years when He was preparing His chosen men for the new things He was planning to do during the next half century.

This kind of secret preparation is not unusual. Often in the darkest hour of a nation's history, there is divine preparation of new instruments of His choosing. Out of the Dark Ages in Europe came new light, new men, and reformation within and without the organized church. Throughout the years, men and women, not institutions or organizations, have been God's method. While our nation's mighty political, economic, and religious oak trees had fallen, the Lord caused a grove of young saplings to spring up in the hinterlands.

While Dawson Trotman was being nurtured as a young sprout in southern California, the heavenly horticulturist had His saplings springing up all over the continent. C. Stacey Woods was helping to organize the U.S. branch of Inter-Varsity Christian Fellowship in Canada, an evangelistic and discipleship ministry to university students that was to become worldwide in its scope and influence; Jim Rayburn was in training in Dallas, Texas, for the leadership of Young Life Campaign, his ministry with high school students; Billy Graham had come off the farm in North Carolina to get his start as a pastor and radio evangelist; and later, out of the ranch land of central Oklahoma came Bill Bright to get tooled up on the campus of UCLA near Los-Angeles for his worldwide outreach with Campus Crusade. Other trees of God's planting during this same time were Dick and Don Hillis, Torrey Johnson, Cliff Barrows, V.R. Edman, Dave Morken, Hubert Mitchell, Charles Fuller, Bob Pierce, Henrietta Mears, Jack Wyrtzen, Bob Evans, Theodore Epp, Lewis Talbot, plus hundreds of pastors, educators, church leaders, and missionaries.

Many of these men and women were close friends and comrades of Dawson Trotman. Every one of them was a "gap" man or woman for God— the kind of servant spoken of in Ezekiel 22:30: "I sought for a man among them, that should make up the hedge, and stand in the *gap* before me for the land, that I should not destroy it: but I found none."

Ezekiel 22:23-29 told the same story in 600 B.C. that newspapers were telling in the days of Dawson Trotman. The prophets, the priests, the princes, and the people had left their moorings. Few had a heart for God. Whereas in Israel, God could find no "gap" men except Ezekiel, in the English-speaking world, He was raising up a whole band of men in the early part of the twentieth century "to make up the hedge and to stand in the gap." These men had few organizational ties to each other, no membership, and no denominational uniformity. They were all evangelicals, and they were all members of a team for God. They would say with united voice, in the words of C.T. Studd: "If Jesus Christ be God, and died for me, then no sacrifice can be too great for me to make for Him."

A divided heart can never bring complete satisfaction. The man of mingled interests will seldom make a success of anything. If he would succeed in business he must give the major portion of his time and the best of his thought to his business. . . . The very same is true of the man who would be used of God, only to a far greater degree. The work alone must claim his whole attention. He has no room for other things.

OSWALD J. SMITH

Chapter 2

An Earthen Vessel

Dawson Trotman did not fit into the traditional "churchly" image of a saint. He was natural, fun-loving, and thoroughly unconventional. He was not a schoolman, deliberately avoided formal ordination to the ministry, had no homiletics to speak of, and possessed an instinctive distrust of tradition. He approached practically all procedures without presuppositions.

That a matter had always been dealt with in a

certain way was no reason, he felt, why it should continue to be dealt with that way. It was, in fact, probably a good reason for striking out in some new direction. He was unimpressed by established precedent, and was not intimidated if his course of action did not receive the approval of traditionalists. When he had figured out the true nature of a problem, he would set himself to find its solution by the exercise of prayer and common sense.

Dawson was unconsciously flamboyant. The statement, "It can't be done" stirred him mightily to prove that it *could* be done. Whether he was interested in a missionary project, committed to a city-wide crusade with the Billy Graham Evangelistic Association, or running a remodeling program for The Navigators' headquarters, he did it with all his might and resources, both his own and that of the top talent he could enlist. Dawson seldom did anything by halves. He was inventive; he rapidly appreciated the difficulties of a situation, and he gave often simple and unsophisticated solutions. If he could not untie knots, he would cut them!

Such an approach quite naturally aroused criticism by the established church. Where the critics obviously had a case, Dawson listened and sometimes changed his methods. But where his convictions were strong, or where the critics were misinformed, he first tried to convert the critics, and if that failed, he ignored them and maintained his course.

The English clergyman Richard H. Froude, in writing to his close friend Thomas Carlyle, said of some faultfinders who were constantly expressing disapproval,

> . . . the mists of criticism do hang about a mountain. Men who want no mists must be content with plains and desert. Mists come with mountains. Soon the mists evaporate, and the mountain will stand out in all its grandeur in the morning sunlight. Multitudes will stay in the valley, for there are few who aspire to reach the summit.

Dawson was a "mountain" man. The mists of criticism did hang about him, especially in the early morning of his ministry, but near the end of his life he stood out in the clear sunlight of wide acceptance by other Christian leaders.

An adventurer for God

For Dawson, truth was not just something to be kept in cold storage. He believed in applying biblical truth to everyday life. He felt that since Christianity was founded by a Person who walked where we walk, His followers should be able to relate truth to life in a very down-to-earth fashion.

Dawson was also optimistic. Because he claimed the promises of Scripture, he developed a healthy self-image. He was sure that the God of Abraham, Isaac, and Jacob was going to fulfill the written promises in spite of weaknesses or limitations that might stand in the way. He was a confident and positive man, and yet his confidence was in God; consequently there was a ring of humility to his life.

One church leader described him in these terms: "Dawson appealed to that adventuresome quality within each one of us, daring us to be more than mediocre, ordinary Christians. He had the ability to bring out the best that is within us. There was that quality about Daws that no matter what he was doing, caused him to want to excel. I never felt that he was satisfied with mediocrity in any dimension, whether he was playing a game of touch football, memorizing Scripture, preaching a sermon, or motivating others to follow Christ."

A practical joker

Dawson had a rare sense of humor. He loved to play tricks on the uninitiated and then bring them into the fellowship of fun. For example, as the Trotman family and guests sat down to dinner at 509 Monterey Road in South Pasadena, a bell would sometimes ring during a lull in the conversation. Dawson would say to one of the newcomers, "Charley, would you mind going to the front door to see who is there?" Charley, surprised by the request, would excuse himself from the dinner table and go to the front door. Finding no one there, he would return to the dining room, only to hear another ring. Daws would then send him to the back door, suggesting it was a special delivery letter. Charley would find his way through the kitchen to the back door, only to find *again* that there was no one there. Back to the table Charley would come, this time amid a roar of laughter. Only then did Dawson show him the button under the table that was used for the initiation ceremony.

His practical jokes loosened up many a "serious" Christian, but sometimes he risked rebuke by going too far. For instance, he often sported a flower on his coat lapel that squirted water into the eye of the unwitting person who had leaned over to "smell the fragrance." There was also the firecracker in the umbrella routine. The firecracker, hidden in the top, would explode when the umbrella was opened. Many a time someone's studied composure would crack under this irreverent treatment, and he would temporarily "lose the victory."

Dawson could tell a joke well, and he seldom used canned stories. He could also take a joke, but that was more difficult.

Informal joshing was his style. He liked to tease, and he was full of good-natured banter. This little anecdote from Clyde Taylor, general director of the National Association of Evangelicals, shows Dawson's humor at its best: "I remember in Brazil, we had traveled all night, or at least till midnight. We finally arrived at the hotel about 1:00 a.m. and had about four hours of sleep when the switchboard operator called us for the 6:00 a.m. wake-up. Even then it was a hurried hour to get to the other side of town for a breakfast meeting with the local missionaries.

"We did have a brief word of prayer together, and that was the total extent of our devotions, unless Dawson repeated some of his memorized verses to himself as the taxi raced us through the people-thronged streets. During his message that morning, what did Daws do? He used me as an illustration of how we ought to have our quiet time every morning without exception! He turned to me in front of the entire group, and said, 'By the way, Clyde, how much time did you spend in devotions this morning?' Well, I thought to myself, That clever rascal, he knows exactly how much time we spent in devotions . . . we were both so dead tired we could hardly move and he knows that I spent as much time as he did, and that was virtually zero!

"'Why, Dawson,' I replied, 'that's a foolish question for you to ask me, for you know we both spent the same amount of time with the Lord this morning.'

"Dawson just looked at me, smiled and nodded his head as much as to say, 'Just wait, Clyde, I'll get you next time!' You had to be prepared for this sort of roasting, and it was of little concern to Daws whether the outcome was going to be in your favor or not, and very frequently he wouldn't ask unless he was pretty sure it wouldn't be."

A compassionate disciplinarian

Dawson was not only fun-loving, he was also creative—yet disciplined. One Navigator staff member had this beautiful memory: "Daws was always in a hurry. I mean by that, he walked fast. He was down to business, and thus he moved fast, but he never gave me the impression that he was in a hurry to get rid of me, for I felt he did enjoy my company. Although he was hurrying through life to get his mission done, I never got the impression he was too busy for people. 'Busy about the King's business but not too busy for the King's people,' might be the best way to describe him."

But he was also somewhat of a paradox. He was gentle, and yet he could be tough, especially to those closest to him, whom he affectionately called his "Gang." He was hard on phonies, and on those who he felt were playing games with God. Many saw him only as a rugged disciplinarian; and yet he was also the loving father and the tenderhearted disciple-maker. He would praise his men from faraway platforms, but face-to-face he could be very severe about their shortcomings.

One of the staff members recalled the time when he was rebuked severely by Dawson. He had a hard time recovering, but later Daws helped him put it into perspective: "The next time I saw him, he asked me to go for a walk. I'll never forget it, because I wept silently when he put his hand out and said: 'You may hear from others that I think this or that about you, but I ask you not to believe it. If I ever have anything to tell you, I'll tell you straight to your face. If we agree to do that, the Devil will never be able to divide us.' We shook hands on that, and down through the years, that experience has helped me overcome the petty divisions, the jealousies and antagonisms which have a tendency to throw us off our drive to really know Christ and to make Him known."

Dawson did not possess every spiritual gift, nor was he perfect. He himself said, "The Navigators have made probably every mistake in the book at least once." They were mistakes of zeal without knowledge, and knowledge could only come with experience. Administration was not Daws's strong point. He was a pioneer, a pathfinder, and a breaker of new ground on the frontiers of discipleship.

This simple fact explains some of his shortcomings. In Dawson Trotman, the twentieth-century church was introduced to a brilliant strategist; yet his own team in The Navigators often saw him as a frustrated president and director. He was a perfectionist, and he could not stand to see imperfect work done by others. His inability to truly delegate responsibility became a thorn in his flesh.

Daws was not a "super-spiritual" hero, but rather a trailblazer, an explorer for God, and an artist. He was, he recognized, molded out of the same clay as the rest of us. He often would describe himself in the words of 2 Corinthians 4:7: "But we have this treasure in earthen vessels, that the excellency of the power may be of God, and not of us." That is how Dawson saw himself—a common earthenware jar, a perishable container.

A builder of foundations

Although Dawson wasn't much for claiming life verses, he said if he had one, it would be Isaiah 58:12: "And they that shall be of thee shall build the old waste places: thou shalt raise up the foundations of many generations; and thou shalt be called, The repairer of the breach, The restorer of paths to dwell in."

The images of construction and building flooded his mind. Daws saw his ministry as that of a builder —a restorer. He and his men were most comfortable when they were behind the scenes. As we shall see later in this book, he identified with the apostle Paul in 1 Corinthians 3:9-10 as "labourers together with God . . . according to the grace of God which is given unto me, as a wise masterbuilder, I have laid the foundation, and another buildeth thereon." His commission and commitment was to raising up "the foundations of many generations."

A nurseryman

Dawson also saw himself as a nurseryman for God, planting, caring, and pruning young trees for the Creator. In his original and homespun manner, Dawson shared this practical analogy at a conference of Navigator staff in California: "Every new tree begins its life in a flower. When a tree seed begins to grow, a new tree is born. This tree inside a seed is extremely small, but it has all the essential parts needed for a tree—there are the roots, the trunk and a crown. As long as a tree lives, it continues to grow. . . . Animals don't keep growing. Nor do human beings. But God has it so planned that trees are ever-growing. That's why I like Isaiah 61:3: 'that they might be called trees of righteousness, the planting of the Lord, that he might be glorified.' We are trees for God. Physically we stop growing, but spiritually, once we are planted by the Lord, we keep on growing till we die.

"What do you want to be, a tree with a little fruit on it, or would you like to be a tree from which is propagated many orchards, until fruit is exported across the seas by the shipload because of you . . . the planting of the Lord, that He might be glorified?"

A passionate heart

To hear Daws preach was thrilling. He often started "chasing rabbits" with stories and illustrations, but he never missed his point. When he was finished, his auditors felt like the disciples in Luke 24:32: "Were not our hearts burning within us while he talked with us . . . and opened the Scriptures to us?" (*The New International Version*).

Dawson Trotman never sought the crowd's approval, nor the corporate crown, but he did seek the Lord with all his heart. He often referred to Jeremiah 45:5: "Seekest thou great things for thyself? Seek them not."

He could minister to crowds as well as to individuals. In the pulpit or speaking at conferences, seminaries, and universities, Daws was a man of world vision. Yet out of that pulpit and down in the dining room, alongside a mountain stream, or in a lawn chair on a cabin porch, he could give an individual his full and undivided attention and love.

Do you know why I often ask Christians, "What's the biggest thing you've asked God for this week?" I remind them that they are going to God, the Father, the Maker of the Universe. The One who holds the world in His hands. What did you ask for? Did you ask for peanuts, toys, trinkets, or did you ask for continents? I want to tell you, young people, it's tragic! The little itsy-bitsy things we ask of our Almighty God. Sure, nothing is too small—but also nothing is too big. Let's learn to ask for our big God some of those big things He talks about in Jeremiah 33:3: "Call unto Me and I will answer thee, and show thee great and mighty things that thou knowest not."

DAWSON TROTMAN

Chapter 3

An Unquenchable Thirst

After his commitment to Christ in 1926, Dawson was consumed with the desire to know God. Many people and organizations played strategic roles in helping him realize that desire. His home church influenced him greatly, both the pastor and his high school teachers Misses Mills and Thomas, who, along with his mother, had "prayed Dawson into the Kingdom." Daws frequently gave his testimony at the Fisherman's Club, the Bible Institute of Los

Angeles, and Christian Endeavor. There were dozens of godly men and women who gave him "a nudge Godward."

But the most significant influence on him was his own personal time alone with his Savior. For though he outwardly appeared to be strong and self-sufficient, inwardly Daws was utterly dependent on God. He spent many hours in Bible study, prayer, memorization, and systematic working through of the great doctrines of Scripture, "building himself up in the most holy faith."

Dawson's theology of God was exciting. He reveled in God's greatness, His holiness, His power, His sovereignty, His grace, His love for all mankind. He spent hours in Genesis 1-3 discovering the God of Creation, and in Genesis 12 discovering how Abraham, the father of the Jewish nation, gained his view of Jehovah God. He devoted extensive time to the major prophets, finding out what they had to say to their own times as well as what they predicted for the future. He loved the message of the four gospels.

His view of God was *big!* One of his staff members said, "I was impressed with Daws's life and the ways he walked in reality with God, his faith, and the way that God seemed to answer his prayers in a very direct way. Here was a man who had personal contact with God. God was very real to him. He might have been small in stature, but he was mighty with God."

Daws believed that humility and faithfulness were prerequisites for knowing God. Speaking to a group of Navigators at Mount Hermon, a well-known Christian conference center near Santa Cruz, California, he said, "The greatest man I know, who has accomplished anything for God—it wasn't because he was smart. It wasn't just because he had a fine education. It was because he was a faithful man. He was a man who had set his face like a flint and he knew that God was bigger than he was. God could do all that He had promised for him and through him. And that man just obeyed God down to the smallest details, and in turn, he let God do whatever He pleased to do. Perhaps God is speaking to some of you. Is there a man sixty years old here? Have you crossed your name off of God's 'I'm Going to Do It through You' list? I've got news for you. The man who started the Fisherman's Club and the Bible Institute of Los Angeles was a man sixty years old. He had six young fellows from Los Angeles, and out of that prayer meeting came the club and the school. God can use you. He wants to use you. God can use that experience when given to Him.

"Whenever I talk to a person about serving God, he so often will say, 'But, Mr. Trotman, I'm so weak and unqualified.' I reply, 'You're a candidate if you're willing to pray and believe.'

"What's *your* excuse? God has an answer to all the excuses of man. Give them to Him, would you?

Tell Him tonight that He is big enough and the job is big enough and that you are going to volunteer. Tell Him. . . . He'll do it."

A man of prayer

These were the years of Dawson's life when the Holy Spirit removed the veil from his eyes to see the power in a life of prayer. Often, in later years, Daws was questioned by young people as to how much time he spent with the Lord in prayer. Here is a typical response: "I don't think *time* has much to do with whether God *hears* me or not. But, I do believe that time has everything to do with *whether my faith is built up* as I pray and as I stretch out in asking. I don't believe that God will ever give those great and mighty things of Jeremiah 33:3 to those who just have their little conscience-easers or some quick prayers before jumping into bed for the night.

"I don't think God has anything big for you if you can't take 1/48th of your day to be alone with your Almighty God and Father. I rather doubt whether He is going to do very much for you."

Although he spent much time in private prayer, Dawson was never a loner in prayer. He loved his time of solitude in a secret place, but he also thoroughly enjoyed fellowship with other men. He could pray with someone by the hour, and often there were all-night prayer meetings. He often challenged us to get alone with God, and "pray,

pray, and pray some more, till you have made sure that all the ground in your life has been covered that needed His forgiveness, anointing, and divine touch."

He delighted to be on his knees with men of God. Daws recalled, "The times of prayer in the early morning in downtown Los Angeles were blessed. We prayed together for two straight years—Bob Munger, Dick and Don Hillis, Rudy Atwood, and Roy Creighton of Christian Endeavor. Every Thursday morning we would meet from 5:00 till 7:00. We prayed for our city of Los Angeles, youth problems, the children of all our families, and then we'd march in prayer across our country—really meeting with God—and always end up praying for world evangelism. Real rugged foundational stones were laid down in my life as we prayed for the city, the nation, and then the uttermost parts of the world."

In his early years of walking with God prayer became the pattern of Dawson's life. His journal is full of reflections and soul-searchings: "Had a truly blessed time alone with the Lord early this morning. Again I have had the matter of *prayer* brought definitely to my attention as being vitally connected with accomplishing much business with God. I set my face again to pursue and persevere in habits of *much time with Him*. Truly, our more difficult work, as refreshing and as wonderful as it is . . . is prayer!"

Daws also wrote in his journal at the time, "We had a wonderful meeting at San Pedro. Afterwards,

Ed, Bill, Jim, Walt and I had a prayer meeting lasting until about 11:00 p.m. A couple of the fellows left, and so Jim, Walt, and I continued all night in prayer to God."

The next day he met again with five men and had a prayer meeting on the hill, then went to Harbor City and preached. It was Friday, August 30. "Went to the old church about 9:00 p.m. and prayed until I could stay awake no longer. Lay down on the floor and slept until daybreak, at which time I again poured out my heart before the Lord."

Years later he had this same prayer burden. Daws was on a missionary survey trip through South America with Clyde Taylor, who observed, "I was tremendously affected by his prayer life. At times on the trip, when we were just about ready for bed after a tiring and busy day, Daws would say, 'Clyde, I think a couple hours with the Lord is what I need right now,' and he would take off into the night. I knew that he would come back perhaps a few hours later, after being alone, and it would show up in his life that next day with a new touch, a fresh devotion, and a sharper hold on the Scriptures. Daws couldn't function without this infusion. He seemed to be able to function without sleep, but not without protracted times in prayer."

Daws wrote dozens of prayer promises upon the tablet of his heart. The quiver of his innermost being was loaded with arrows with which he could reach the heart of God. These portions of Scripture, along with the influence of godly people, gave him his sense of urgency in prayer.

Among the chief influences in those early Christian years were books that he almost memorized because of their Bible-centered quality. Books by Hudson Taylor, George Mueller, and E.M. Bounds were his diet. These men were much with God, and their example stimulated Dawson to a deeper life of prayer.

Perhaps no one statement, aside from Scripture, had greater influence on his praying than this short paragraph from the classic, *Power Through Prayer*, by E.M. Bounds:

> Men are God's method. The Church is looking for better methods; God is looking for better men. . . . What the Church needs today is not more machinery or better, nor new organizations or more and novel methods, but men whom the Holy Ghost can use—men of prayer, men mighty in prayer. The Holy Ghost does not . . . come on machinery, but on men. He does not anoint plans, but men—men of prayer.

A growing eagerness to trust God
But giants in prayer and faith are not born that way; they have to grow. It took Dawson nearly thirty years to become a seasoned veteran.

His new life in Christ began when he was twenty years old. At first his faith was as small as a mustard seed. Daws started off by trusting God for fifty cents for carfare and for the food that he and Lila would need for their family and for all the sailors who daily arrived in the small home in the harbor area of Los Angeles. It was many years before he dared to believe God in prayer for fifty dollars, and long after that before he asked the Lord for $110,000 in a six-week time period in order to purchase a new headquarters in Colorado. Caleb's faith, expressed in Numbers 13:30, "Let us go up at once, and possess it; for we are well able to overcome it," was twenty-seven years in maturing for Dawson.

Dawson's faith spread out in continually widening circles, like the waves from a pebble dropped in a pool of water. He first trusted God for the salvation of his neighbors, employers, and friends in Lomita and Long Beach, California before he trusted Him for the salvation of people throughout the United States and nations of the world.

He and his wife Lila grew in their faith together. But they did more than that. As they began to believe God for greater things, they took other men and women along with them on the path of faith. Because they fed on the promises of Almighty God, they were able to feed others and to show them how to feed themselves.

As Dawson's confidence and trust grew, he

developed a pattern of "risk-taking," acting in faith before God had actually supplied the money, and this lifestyle began to become evident in the people associated with him in the ministry.

Most important, he never quit! He gathered around him men who trusted God as well. It was a team effort: Dawson and God; Dawson, Lila, and God; Dawson, his family, his "Gang" of colaborers, and God. The wider his circle of influence spread, the more his faith grew to nurture the added responsibility. It was not a one-way street. He was also stimulated by the faith of his growing team. Together they diligently sought God, convinced that "He that cometh to God must believe that he is, and that he is a rewarder of them that *diligently* seek him" (Hebrews 11:6).

During the latter part of the summer of 1948 Dawson saw a dramatic answer to prayer. The first Youth for Christ World Congress on Evangelism was being held at a Bible school in Beatenberg, Switzerland. Representatives of youth groups from every major country in the world were there. Some of the leaders sensed an undercurrent of animosity and bitterness between groups from various nations. There was deep spiritual concern.

After lunch one day, four of the men, Bob Evans, Hubert Mitchell, Billy Graham, and Dawson Trotman, got off into a spot on the mountainside where they could pour out their hearts to one another and to God. Daws told the story: "Before we prayed, we had a confessional meeting. We all felt that we wanted to have power in our lives, more quickening of God's Holy Spirit, a greater knowledge of His Word, and we just wanted to be earthen vessels that were clean and pure and strong to do the will of God.

"We made a covenant on that mountainside, and the four of us stood there like the four corners of the earth and we shook hands across, four pairs of hands, and we formed the cross and made a contract together that from that moment on we would give ourselves to the Word, prayer, and the preaching of the gospel to the ends of the earth!"

God heard and answered their prayers. All four men have been used in significant ways of leadership for the kingdom of God—Bob Evans, the visionary leader of Greater Europe Mission in Europe; Hubert Mitchell, pioneer missionary leader in India and Indonesia; Billy Graham, servant of God in worldwide evangelism; and Dawson Trotman, founder of The Navigators and discipler of men. It would be a fascinating study to discover how God brought each of those four men to that spiritual altar in Switzerland where the wood of man and the flame of God broke into white heat. What God did for these four men in answer to prayer, He also did for the entire delegation at the Congress. God moved in mightily!

There is no doubt that Dawson was, at this period of his life, on the growing edge of a life of faith in God—whether it concerned his class of six Sunday school boys, his personal finances, his married life with beloved Lila, his own fledgling team of co-workers, or a ministry with men on a mountainside in Switzerland.

Prayer was serious business with Daws, because he took God seriously. Former Navigator Vice President Jim Downing related an incident that illustrates this attitude. "The last conference in which I participated with him was out in Honolulu in 1953. I remember we got up early in the morning to have devotions, and he went into Psalm 103 and said to me, 'Jim, I've got to confess this early in the morning that I have been awake for over half an hour and I haven't asked God for anything great yet.' Dawson felt that he had literally wasted thirty minutes of that day!"

Daws committed the first couple of hours of each day to finding out what God had on His mind for those particular twenty-four hours. "Lord, what's on Your heart, for that is what I want on my heart." Then, after searching the Scriptures, praying for illumination and insight, and making sure that "all was clean and confessed up," Dawson was ready for action. Because he took God at His Word, he believed the promises he had memorized, he prayed over them and wrote his name into them, and then moved out into day-by-day production. He expressed it to his staff like this: "You've got to believe. Believe the Bible. Believe in God. Believe that whatever He has said, He will do. And then you have to swing into action. You can't do what *God* wants to do, but on the other hand, God isn't going to do what He is asking *you* to do. Before you can touch people in forty-eight states, you've got to believe and ask to touch people in one state. Before that happens, you've got to believe and ask God for folks in one city, but all that is the result of believing and asking God for your neighbors on one street. I believe that every Christian is a potential witness, but it must begin on his or her street. Do you believe that?"

This reality in prayer is one of the secrets to Dawson's spiritual life. He focused on the living God and His willingness and power to fulfill His promises. Because of his faith, his life served as an example and challenge not only to his generation, but to all of us who follow.

Daws was so saturated with the Word of God in his early Christian life through memorizing Scriptures and trying to apply them to his everyday living that he actually personalized the promises. With all his being, Dawson felt that from what God had promised Abraham, he could claim a personal application for himself. Even if the promises weren't written *to* him, they surely were written *for* him. Dawson's own journey through the library of Scripture gave him a conviction that "all the promises are mine," and that "by faith, I am going to step out on each and every one I can!"

He claimed these promises for himself, as well as for world evangelization. He was absolutely sure that God was going to fulfill them in spite of whatever weaknesses might exist, or whatever impossible circumstances might stand in the way. He loved to repeat, "Faith grows but by exercise, in circumstances impossible!"

Problems don't come too big for God

There weren't too many positive things going for Daws in the first twenty years of his life. Poor health, a weak body, and shady friendships were constantly pulling him downward. Yet during the last thirty years of his life, Dawson was a confident man, a positive thinker, an inspiration to thousands, and an enthusiastic exhorter.

All spiritual leaders feel their own shortcomings keenly. Daws was no exception. Because he recognized his human weakness, Dawson also recognized the absolute necessity for divine help. He felt that God must have complete control of his life. "Not I, but Christ" was his theme. Because he believed God's promise in Jeremiah 33:3 to answer those who call upon Him, the word "impossible" was not in his vocabulary. Hadn't God Himself made the statement and asked the question, "Behold, I am the Lord, the God of all flesh: is there anything too hard for me?" (Jeremiah 32:27).

One of the many times when God did the impossible occurred on an international trip. Dawson was heading for Calcutta, India, with his close missionary friend Dick Hillis. They were due to preach in the William Carey Church of Calcutta, but because of the cancellation of a Pan American flight, the two men were stranded in Bangkok, Thailand. They got down on their knees there in the hotel room and prayed, "Lord, this is an impossible situation, so we are asking You to take over. Right now, we are going to thank You for what is going to happen in the next couple of hours. Thank You!"

Arriving at the airport they got word that a plane was flying in from Manila and Hong Kong, but it was not going any farther that day. They asked the clerk why it wasn't completing its scheduled flight on to India. "Well, Mr. Trotman, we have international flight regulations that tell us no crew can fly three shifts—that would be dangerous." Daws and Dick looked at each other, nodded in agreement and went over to a quiet spot in the terminal and again talked to God. "Lord, with You there are no international rules or red tape. We will leave it with You to work it all out so we can be in Calcutta on schedule."

Then came the not-so-surprising radio message instructing the same crew to fly their Pan-Am ship on to Calcutta immediately. There were only four passengers on that plane, and Daws and Dick were the only ones who had to arrive by a definite hour! As the plane cleared the waterways and the Buddhist temples of the city of Bangkok, these men offered up a word of thanksgiving: "Thank You, Lord; You indeed are in charge."

Dawson's closing remarks to that story are classic: "Problems don't come too big for God. He can do anything He wants to do, and anything anyone wants to have done—in accordance with His overall will—He wants to do.

He would go on to say, "The need of the hour, as far as I'm concerned, is for people to believe that God is God. He is far more interested in getting His job done than we are in doing it. He has all power to do it. He has commissioned *us* to do it. Therefore, can we not trust Him for everything we need to get the job done?

"Gang, circumstances change; our situations change; our outlooks change; our dreams fade; our ideas are lost; but with God, nothing changes. God has a plan and He has been working on it for thousands of years right on schedule. God visualized the Cross of Calvary before the foundations of the world. From eternity, God knew that His Son, the Lord Jesus Christ, would be the Lamb that one day would take away the sin of the world. He knew it, but didn't share it openly with His men. How foolish the prophets of the Old Testament must have felt in writing some of the things they wrote. But they didn't know or didn't understand fully the heart of God. Moses must have felt that way: 'Why am I writing things that I don't even understand?'

"And then the word came to Joshua, who was to take Moses' place in leadership, and God said, 'As I was with Moses, I will be with you.' Now, what did Joshua have on you and me? Gang, we've got something on Joshua. Joshua never had a copy of the Old Testament. Joshua never had a Bible concordance. Joshua never had electric lights. Joshua never had central heating. But there is one thing that Joshua had and that we have—God's Word and God's presence."

The experience of Daws's attitude of faith took place in the crucible of Jeremiah 33:3: "Call unto me, and I will answer thee, and shew thee great and mighty things, which thou knowest not." The little 1¾ by 2¾ inch white card that had this memory verse printed upon it was well worn and dog-eared as Dawson reviewed and meditated upon it day after day. Did God really mean those three things mentioned in that verse?

1. Call upon me.
2. I will answer you.
3. I will show you great and mighty things.

These words were to launch Daws, with bulldog-like tenacity, into an experience which he has called, "the turning point of my life."

The turning point

Dawson asked his good friend Walt if he believed those words from the prophet Jeremiah about calling to God and having answers that were never before seen. When Walt hesitantly said, "I guess so," Dawson's reply was, "Well, so do I, Walt, and I've never seen it happen, but I'd sure like to."

The two men began a search of Scripture on the subject of prayer, with Jeremiah 33:3 as the foundation. How do you stake a claim on the promises of God? What are some of the basic ingredients of making sure God will answer? What about the subject of "importunity" mentioned in Luke 11:8? What does the Bible teach about the time of day, the position of the body, and the attitude of the heart in prayer?

The answers to these questions, along with a host of others, were flooding the hearts of Walt and Daws as they covenanted to pray together every morning until they felt assured that God was going to fulfill His promise in their lives.

Beginning that very week, early in the day before the sun came up, they rode out to a canyon near their homes, built a fire, and knelt in prayer. With open Bibles, they began to pray by name for the boys God had given them through their Sunday school and Boys' Club ministry. For two hours each morning they brought their requests to God, pausing only to reread from the Bible the great and precious promises that spurred them on when they felt their prayers were going nowhere. Often they would break up grudgingly, in order to get to work by 8:00 a.m. On Sunday morning, they met and prayed for three hours.

Dawson recalled that as the days passed, "we prayed for Harbor City and Torrance and Long Beach and San Pedro and Los Angeles and Pasadena and then the surrounding cities. I had received calls from Christian leaders and pastors asking us to come over to their churches and show them how they could reach young boys.

"The third and fourth weeks we began extending our prayer interests up the West Coast—San Francisco, Oakland, Portland, and Seattle."

Daws and Walt decided that if God could answer prayer right where they lived in southern California, He surely could do it in other places too.

Day after day these two men brought before the Lord promises they claimed from the Bible, especially pledges and contracts the Lord made in Isaiah and Jeremiah.

While these promises were soaking in their souls, God began giving them faith to believe that He was going to enable them to reach for Christ men from all of the forty-eight states. They started praying for men from Washington, Oregon, Texas, Illinois, and then throughout the eastern U.S. on down to Florida.

Dawson continued: "I don't know which one of us suggested that we get a map of the world, for that surely would give us a good prayer list for weeks to come. We bought a world map with all the nations in beautiful color and would leave it up there in the hills, covered up at night with a piece of old canvas. Each morning we would roll it out and put our fingers on China, Japan, a little island called Formosa, and the Philippines. As we moved in our prayer time, we started praying for Greece, the island of Cyprus, Egypt, and the countries of Africa. What exciting days as we covered the world in our intercession, praying by name for each nation and asking, 'God, allow us to serve You some day in each of these places and enable us to reach men for You in every one of these continents of the world.'"

At the end of forty-two days, they felt the burden lift, and they began to thank God that He had heard them and was going to fulfill what He had promised. During the six weeks they had spent over one hundred hours in prayer in the hills together with God, asking Him to use them to win and train men for His glory around the world. Little did they realize what was in store for them in the years to come!

Many years later, while looking through some papers in a drawer, Daws found a purple card with "Washington" written on it, and under it was the name of a sailor from that state won to Christ through Daws's witness. There were other names—Les from Illinois, John from Texas, Ed from Wisconsin. Daws and Lila discovered that evening that men from every one of the forty-eight states had been touched by their ministry. Jeremiah 33:3 had been partially fulfilled.

Looking back on those forty-two days of prayer, Dawson remarked, "In those days, we were just saying, 'Okay, Lord, bring us into touch with men. Bring them to us.' We didn't even know what we were praying. I didn't realize that within four years, men from every state of the nation would walk into our front room and find the Savior. God answered our prayers abundantly, and there was the beginning of our work called today by the name, Navigators."

The end of that forty-two-day prayer meeting marked a turning point in the life of this man who believed God. It did not come about by attending a conference or seminar, nor by hearing a sermon on faith or prayer, nor by seeing great results through preaching to audiences of thousands. It came, rather, by the exercise of personal faith in God's promises, and through gradually believing God for even greater things.

That turning point in Daws's life came when he made a covenant with God to believe God's promises and to intercede for men. Daws believed that this kind of prayer was not the privilege of a select few, but the right and responsibility of every Christian. His only regret later in life was, "I only wish that I had asked God for more!"

*For Ezra had prepared his heart
to seek the law of the Lord, and
to do it, and to teach in Israel
statutes and judgments.*

EZRA 7:10

*If you mean business for God,
at the center of your life must
be Jesus Christ.*

DAWSON TROTMAN

Chapter 4

At the Heart of Life

The night air grew cooler in the Hollywood hills as Dawson Trotman let the final spoke of a mechanical wheel spring into place. It was late, but his young audience sat entranced. They could see the spoke clearly: WITNESSING. This was the wrap-up of a fascinating evening in which Daws had explained how to live a successful Christian life—a life which he called "Christ-centered" and "Spirit-filled." The mechanical wheel contained a rim, a hub, and four spokes. Dawson's visual aid was the result of his efforts to make the truths of the Christian life understandable to those he was teaching. More than any other symbol, The Wheel has come to be known as the distinctive Navigator illustration of discipleship.

Living a balanced life

What is The Wheel, and how did it come to stand for the Christ-centered, Spirit-filled life? To find the answer to that question one has to go to the book that was one of Daws's early favorites, *The Seven Laws of Teaching*, by John M. Gregory.

Gregory's fundamental rule was, "Begin with what is already well known to the pupil upon the subject and with what he has himself experienced, and proceed to the new material by single, easy and natural steps, letting the known explain the unknown." Daws's own illustrations were always subject to revision in order to make the truth of Scripture clearer and more practical in everyday life.

The Wheel illustration began as a three-legged stool during Daws's days of teaching his boys' Sunday school class at a church in Lomita. He had heard an illustration that likened the Christian life to a stool with three legs—the Bible, Prayer, and Witnessing. If any one of the three legs was missing, the stool couldn't stand up by itself.

Dawson described the illustration's transition from a stool to a wheel: "As I thought about the stool, I didn't like the illustration, because the Christian life shouldn't be lived sitting down! A stool is great if you are milking a cow, repairing a shoe, or peeling potatoes. Christians aren't sitting—especially little boys.

"I began to think of a three-spoked wheel, because a wheel is something a boy or a grown man can identify with. Automobiles, bicycles, ships, and trains all use wheels.

"*The hub had to be Christ.* The rim had to be the well-rounded Christian, living his life in the power of the Holy Spirit. But what about the spokes? I found my boys could learn their Bible verses, they could pray, and they could witness to their buddies, but something was wrong. There was something missing. We needed a fourth spoke, which we called 'Living the Life.' Later we called it simply 'Obedience.'

"Now the wheel made sense. It was balanced with two vertical spokes and two horizontal spokes. These were the four basics of the Christian life, with the Lord Jesus Christ right in the middle. If any one of the four is missing or is out of proportion, the entire wheel gets off balance and you have a lop-sided Christian who is going *thump, thump, thump* down through life. Ezra 7:10 gives us this picture: prayer—Ezra prepared his heart; the Word—to seek the law of the Lord; obedience—and to do it; witnessing—and to teach in Israel statutes and judgments."

Ezra seemed to Daws to be a well-rounded,

godly man, effecting change in his generation because of these four basic elements that were rooted in his life.

As this illustration increasingly became the identifying mark of Dawson and The Navigators, he was asked to preach it from pulpits and platforms around the world. To assist visually in the presentation, a layman in California made a mechanical wheel for Daws to carry with him. It collapsed into a small unit so it would easily fit into his briefcase, and he could carry it in his hand with a Bible. He even carried it to China and had the Chinese characters written on the spokes!

It was this mechanical wheel that Dawson was holding that night in Hollywood when I first heard him present this message. There was nothing inside the rim, just a tire on the circumference that had the lettering, THE SPIRIT-FILLED CHRISTIAN LIVING THE LIFE. Those seven words were circling the rim. Daws would hold this contraption in his left hand high enough so we could all see it, and then ask, "What are the component parts that will give this wheel driving, guiding, and holding power? What do we need inside of this circle called 'Christian' in order for this man or woman to be a producer for God? Come on, gang, mention some things that are absolutes—bedrock essentials if this person is going to grow and mature in Christ."

From all over the audience came the suggestions: "The Bible . . . the church . . . confession . . . the Holy Spirit . . . prayer . . . soulwinning . . . fellowship . . . the Great Commission . . . tithing . . . Scripture memory . . ." and at least another dozen ideas. Daws wrote these all down on a huge blackboard behind him on the stage. The list contained probably twenty-five items.

"Okay, kids," Daws continued, "sit there now and concentrate on these suggestions. Can you sift out the fundamental four or five? Which of these are the imperatives?"

Daws let us sit there for a few minutes while he picked up the mechanical wheel, got it positioned in his left arm, and then remarked, "Let me help you along. Look over here now. Forget the blackboard and that list of ideas. Suppose this wheel is your life. You know that Christ is your Savior, and to the best of your ability you want to start moving for God. Desperately you want more than anything else in life to bring glory to His name. What do you need?"

He pulled a little wire lever on the side of the Wheel, and out popped a white hub smack in the middle, with one word painted on it—CHRIST! "There it is, young people," said Dawson. "If you mean business for God, at the center of your life must be Jesus Christ. That is why Paul told the little congregation in Philippi, 'For to me to live is Christ.' Even though Paul was in prison at the time, the central thrust of his life was Christ. From this hub comes your driving power, your guiding power, and your holding power. The hub is attached to the axle, which is attached to the drive shaft, and hence, to the motor. Because Christ is at the heart of the Christian's life, we are called Christ-ones, or Christians. The local tab may be Presbyterians or Lutherans, but we are all in Christ, and therefore, all Christians. From Him comes our life, our power to be victorious, and our all-sufficiency.

"Try to put anyone else's name in this little white circle, and it wouldn't work. Put your father's name, your pastor's name, the greatest Bible teacher or church saint you may know or have ever heard about, and if that person is at the hub of your life, you've got problems."

Dawson put the Wheel back on the pulpit, got back to the blackboard, and after erasing the list of suggestions, called out for Scripture references that indicate that Jesus Christ is the hub of the Christian life. Starting with Colossians 1:18, "that in all things he might have the preeminence," the list began to grow: Philippians 3:10, John 14:6, Ephesians 3:14-15, and Revelation 1:8.

With a flick of his finger, Dawson released the catch, and the first two of the four spokes swung down into place, connecting the hub to the rim. In his characteristically dramatic style, he showed that the two spokes of the wheel that tie the Christian into a living relationship with Christ are the Word and prayer: "In the Word of God, He speaks to us, and in prayer, we speak to Him. These perpendicular spokes are the two means of grace that have been given so that we can have fellowship with God. The Bible and prayer are foundational to a Christ-centered life.

"Which is the most important? They both are. Which do you need most, food or air? Both are essential to keep on living. It isn't either-or; it is both-and. A newborn baby needs to breathe, and it needs its mother's milk. Which is more important to a new babe in Christ—the Word or prayer? He needs them both, but we put the spoke entitled THE WORD here on the bottom, for it is so essential to all the rest.

"In my own experience, it was out of the Bible that I learned about prayer. One of the first verses that I memorized on how to grow as a new Christian was John 16:24—'Hitherto have ye asked nothing in my Name: ask and ye shall receive, that your joy may be full.' I would never have known that if it wasn't for the Word of God. Because He said it, I believed it and started acting upon it. It is a promise of God. Where did I get it? From the Bible. That's why I have placed THE WORD here on the bottom as the foundational spoke.

"But would you notice, young people, that both THE WORD and PRAYER are linked with CHRIST in the center. Without Him, you don't really know the power of God in the Bible nor the power of God through prayer. 'As newborn babes, desire the sincere milk of the word, that ye may grow thereby'—1 Peter 2:2. But we must never forget that Matthew 7:7 was also given to baby Christians: 'Ask, and it shall be given unto you; seek, and ye shall find; knock, and it shall be opened unto you.'

"If it be true that every person born into this world needs food and air for breathing, can you think of anything else that might be essential?"

Dawson was fishing for ideas that would fit into the blank spaces on the mechanical wheel. He reminded his audience that the next two spokes would be placed horizontally. Since the first two spokes represented the basis of the Christian's relationship with God, these last two symbolized his relationship with men. Living the Christian life demanded "good health" and "exercise." To emphasize his point Daws pulled another lever hidden in the back, and another spoke fell into place—OBEDIENCE. He then asked everyone with Bibles to turn to Psalm 119:59-60—"I thought on my ways, and turned my feet unto thy testimonies. I made haste, and delayed not to keep thy commandments." Dawson commented, "Would you notice the *personal* action taken by David in this song? *I* thought, *I* turned my feet, *I* made haste, *I* delayed not to keep. Hundreds of times throughout the Scriptures, we are not only advised, but *commanded* to obey the words of God. This is the secret of the Christ-centered, Spirit-filled life. Stay away from diseases that you know will put you out of commission for God. Avoid yielding to Satan's temptation. The life of victory in Christ is this spoke of the wheel called OBEDIENCE."

The fourth spoke, of course, was WITNESS-ING, the spiritual exercise of a healthy Christian. Daws observed, "Many folks feel that this final spoke should be called the Church, but I like to remind them that it isn't always possible for people to go to church. Every believer should belong to a local assembly, but for various reasons some don't.

"The church is not just a single spoke; it's the entire Wheel. It's a lot of Wheels working together. Seen up close, this man or woman is a Christ-centered, Spirit-filled Christian. In perspective, that well-rounded, moving individual should have his membership in a local church. But for the believer 'exercise' is not limited to an organization or fellowship group, but is, rather, a whole lifestyle, whether he is in a certain building or not. That's one reason why we call this spoke WITNESSING. It is the responsibility not just of the preacher, the evangelist, or the full-time Christian worker. It is a command given to us all. It is not optional, but imperative."

Driving home to Long Beach that night in 1952, I reflected on all Dawson had said. I reviewed the Wheel and its application to my own life: the four ingredients—Scripture, prayer, obedience, and witnessing. I pondered long and hard on the centrality of

Jesus Christ as the hub of my life. I knew that evening that the results I wanted were out there on the rim—a Christ-centered, Spirit-filled life. Was I willing to set the priorities, establish the goals, and discipline my life to make this Wheel a reality in my life?

Many years previous to that night, my parents had given me a Bible upon graduation from high school. In the front pages they had shared this meditation from the pen of the Episcopal Bishop Phillips Brooks, of Holy Trinity Church, Philadelphia:

> Do not pray for an easy life . . . pray to be a stronger man. Do not pray for tasks equal to your powers; pray for powers equal to your tasks! Then the doing of your work shall be no miracle, but you shall be the miracle. Every day you shall wonder at yourself, at the richness of life which has come to you by the grace of God.

God's Word is your weapon. If you doubt its strength what power can you have in wielding it? It is your only source of information. When the Word of God becomes your meat and drink, your daily study and a very part of yourself, then, and not until then, will you be able to use it as He intends. Do you believe that the text you proclaim is the living, inspired Word of God? And are you confident that it will never return void? God cannot use a man who doubts His Word.

OSWALD J. SMITH

Chapter 5

A Master Swordsman

To understand Dawson Trotman, one has to know that he had a consuming desire to be a man of the Bible and to help others become men and women of the Bible. Daws really had only one string on his guitar, and he would plunk it often and loud: "Let the word of Christ dwell in you richly" (Colossians 3:16). Dawson wanted the Bible to be so at home in his life that he could obey it anywhere and handle it as a master swordsman, wielding the "sword of the Spirit."

Daws simply believed God's Word. Sometimes he believed it so literally that some people called him presumptuous. Some theologians scoffingly interpreted his simple faith as "wrongly dividing the word of Truth." Some men stated both privately and publicly that Trotman was naive and biblically uneducated. But to Daws, the Word of God truly was "a two-edged sword," and was supposed to be used as a personal weapon under the guidance of the Holy Spirit. He handled it both carefully and skillfully.

From pool games to memory verses
Dawson did have a grasp of the Scriptures that was unusual, and he got it largely on his own. He didn't grow up in a godly home (although his mother was a Christian, there was no spiritual nurture there, nor did he attend an evangelical Sunday school and church). He did, however, have a couple of school teachers, Miss Mills and Miss Thomas, who prayed earnestly for his conversion for six years.

Dawson's conversion came when he was twenty—through memorizing Scripture. He had had a run-in with the law, the latest of a series, and he made a promise to God: "Lord, if you will get me out of this trouble with the police, I will go to church this coming Sunday."

As Daws expressed it, "On the Friday night that I was arrested, Miss Mills was home looking up verses in the Bible, trying to find ten on the subject of salvation which she and Miss Thomas could give to the young people in their church group to memorize. Little did she know that the boy for whom they had been praying for six years was going to memorize those verses. When Sunday came along, I decided to go to the young people's meeting. That was a tough decision, for my favorite pool hall was just around the corner—suppose some of the fellows saw me going to church?

"It was the opening night for a contest, and points were to be given for various church activities, among them the memorization of Bible portions. 'Learn ten verses and get fifty points for our side,' said this lovely little blond gal. I went home and dug out my little Testament, and in the course of a week, I had learned all ten verses. Not because it was the Bible, but because of the pretty high school girl! Then they gave me ten more verses . . . on how to grow in the Christian life.

"How they prayed all that week for me! I went back the following Sunday and got another fifty points for the Red team as well as for the little blonde."

Dawson continued with the climax of the story: "One unforgettable event resulted from that contest. . . . I was on my way to work at the local lumber company one day with these twenty verses of Scripture stored away in my memory. I had no plans for using them, except to keep my promise and help win the award for the Reds on the following Sunday.

"I was walking along the highway, minding my own business, with my lunch pail in my hand. Miss Mills was still praying, and the Word of God was working through the power of the Holy Spirit, and all of a sudden that morning, as I walked along to work, one of these twenty verses came into my mind:

'Verily, verily, I say unto you, He that heareth my word, and believeth on him that sent me, hath everlasting life . . .'—John 5:24. Those words, 'hath everlasting life,' stuck in my mind. I said, 'O God, that's wonderful—a person can have everlasting life!' I pulled my little Testament out of my pocket and looked it up in John's Gospel, and sure enough, there it was—'hath everlasting life, and shall not come into condemnation; but is passed from death unto life.'

"There for the first time I remember praying, after I had grown to be a man, 'O God, whatever this means, I want to have it.' That was my new birth. That was the beginning. I believed God and I prayed, and the Lord did all the rest."

Once Dawson became a Christian, he began feeding a voracious appetite for Scripture. "Immediately after my conversion, I began learning more verses from the Bible. I learned one a day for the first three years of my Christian life. I learned my first thousand verses driving a truck for that lumber company in the Harbor area of Los Angeles. A verse a day on that truck, and would you believe—I never ran over anyone with that truck!

"I made up my mind that I was going to get to know the Bible, and I did it. None of this, 'I'll give it a try,' 'I sure hope I can memorize ten verses,' 'I'm not very good at memory but I'll see what I can do.' The point is this, folks, if you say you *will*, then you will *do* it. I'm going to review my Scriptures even if I have to hang by one leg from the chandelier to stay awake."

Little wonder that thirty years later, Dawson Trotman and the Navigator organization were known around the world for their Topical Memory System. One of the seeds planted in Daws's heart was memorizing God's Word, and this practice dominated his early growth. Almost immediately he got busy in his local church, teaching a junior boy's Sunday school class, helping in the activities of Christian Endeavor, and sharing his faith with others in public worship.

He incorporated into his life any and all legitimate ways to absorb the Scriptures. Bible studies with other young men, taking notes on his pastor's sermons, listening to radio programs that featured Bible instruction, a year at the Bible Institute of Los Angeles—these were whetting his appetite for even more. Dawson just couldn't get enough of the Bible. His capacity grew with his intake, and as he grew, he desperately wanted to share these "rich gems" of Scripture with others in southern California.

A love for all of Scripture

The discovery of "hidden treasures" was Dawson's special delight. For example, he went down into the gold mine of 2 Timothy 3:16—4:2 and came up with these nuggets from God:

- All Scripture is given by inspiration of God, and is profitable . . . (3:16)
- That the man of God may be thoroughly furnished unto every good work. (3:17)
- Preach the word . . . in season and out of season. . . . (4:2)

Dawson took 2 Timothy 3:16 to heart. He dissected it, meditated on it, memorized it, and took a good look at its context. Then he went to work to apply it. "All Scripture is profitable." Not just the Old Testament, nor just the Pauline Epistles, nor just the life of Christ found in the four gospels, nor even a few favorite passages like Psalm 23 or the Sermon on the Mount. "All" *meant* "all" to Dawson. It was his obligation to read it all, study it all, and hear, memorize, and meditate on "all Scripture" as much as possible in his lifetime.

This "set of his sail" caused Daws to develop his own system of lay theology. Betty Skinner pointed this out in her biography of Trotman, *Daws*:

He was less drawn to objective analysis of its doctrine than to serious acceptance of its direct meaning to him as a personal message from God. . . . He believed God was promising *him* or commanding *him* or speaking to *him* through a given text. Though the notes in his Scofield Bible defined the successive dispensations, Dawson felt free to take personally a promise or command intended for one of another era in God's timetable.

Dawson especially loved the Old Testament; the poetic beauty of the books made them his delight. He loved to claim promises out of the book of Isaiah. The dating of this tremendous volume or critical views about its authorship did not concern Daws. Neither did it seem wrong to him to take for his own what seemingly belonged to the Israelite nation but was never possessed by them. If they wouldn't claim these promises, Dawson would!

One Old Testament promise became especially precious to both Dawson and Lila in the post World War II days of their marriage. Most of the Navigator work at that time centered in the men of the United States Navy. One sailor in Honolulu was turned off by Dawson's personality and his manner of leadership. He started a vicious smear campaign and sent a lengthy letter to the Navigator mailing list as well as to some prominent church leaders on the West Coast. Those were emotionally draining days.

Daws and Lila together made the decision to move forward for Christ and to keep their mouths shut. One morning during that difficult time, Daws came across Isaiah 54:17. He claimed it in victory for himself, his family, and the ministry, both stateside and in Honolulu: "No weapon that is formed against thee shall prosper; and every tongue that shall rise against thee in judgment thou shalt condemn. This is the heritage of the servants of the Lord, and their righteousness is of me, saith the Lord."

All Scripture is profitable

In many ways, Dawson's was a revolutionary approach to the Scriptures, an approach not taught in many churches, seminaries, or religious circles of his day. Daws didn't get hung up on critical problems of the Old Testament; he just accepted the thirty-nine books as "God-breathed" and went from there. He didn't get stymied on whether promises were to the Jews or to the church, he just took the entire canon of holy writings and asked the Lord to show him a personal application. Some of the passages in the first seventeen books of the Bible opened his eyes to new fields of service and formed the basis of promises he claimed in sending out missionaries to various countries of the world.

A former Navigator staff member and veteran missionary to the Orient looked back with fond memories: "Key passages that some churchmen would feel were obscure and perhaps not to be touched by the church in the twentieth century became foundational for Dawson. He and the Nav team were living by them. This kind of practical application was, in his day, a radical approach to the appropriation of the Word of God."

One incident that illustrates Dawson's use of the Bible in a very practical way occurred in September of 1955. I was privileged to be with Daws in Tokyo for a Navigator staff meeting. At the time, some deep-seated doctrinal problems had surfaced around the person and work of the Holy Spirit, and they had the potential for either splitting the ministry or binding it together even more strongly. The days were long and sleep was hard to come by. I was spending nights on a cot between Dawson and Dick Hillis, Director of Orient Crusades, who was there as an observer and counselor to Daws. My fitful sleep was rudely interrupted one night at about 1:00 a.m. when Daws and Dick got into a pillow fight—and I was right in the middle! The ensuing battle provided a good outlet, releasing emotions and clearing minds through fun, exercise, and some hearty laughs. Only our hosts, the Roy Robertsons, would know about the condition of those pillows!

Our exhilaration subsiding, we turned on the radio to the military overseas station to pick up the World Series game between the Brooklyn Dodgers and the New York Yankees. Soon Hillis was sound asleep, and figuring Dawson was too, I flipped off the radio. I was lying on my back, meditating about all I had seen and heard that day, when Dawson's husky voice quietly broke the stillness: "Hey Bob, you awake?"

"You bet Daws. Just lying here thinking, reflecting and wondering what's going to happen tomorrow. Guess I'm too keyed up to do much sleeping."

"Yeah, me too. Hey, Bob, would you do me a favor and make a little covenant with me? No blood or signing your name—nothing like that."

"Sure, Daws, what do you have in mind?"

"If you ever see me do or say anything out of order, Bob, pull me up short, would you? If you will, get your Bible in the morning and mark it at Proverbs 9:8-9. Put in the margin, 'D.T., Tokyo, 9/29/55.' Reprove not a scorner, lest he hate thee; rebuke a wise man, and he will love thee. Give instruction to a wise man, and he will be yet wiser; teach a just man, and he will increase in learning. If you can do that, I'd sure appreciate it. Good night, fellow. Let's get a little shuteye, okay?"

Sure enough, Daws rolled over on his side and fell sound asleep. I thought I had been keyed up because of the pillow fight, but this time I didn't sleep until I saw the sun slowly coming up over the horizon of Tokyo, Japan.

I never had to follow up on that covenant, for nine months later God took Dawson home to be with Himself. I have often thought about that middle-of-the-night rendezvous with Daws in Tokyo, and about his unique way of making an ancient proverb come alive in our everyday world. But that was no isolated exception. That was daily practice for Dawson. All Scripture is profitable, and he was determined to take God up on all His promises.

Martin Luther left it on record that the correct way of reading the Bible is through a right use of the personal pronouns: "Every promise of God is made to *me*." From the very first day of Daws's commitment to God he had a corresponding commitment to God's book. The Scriptures were supreme in every area of his personal life and they controlled the entire operation of his ministry and outreach. Dawson felt that he was responsible to obey the Word of God, regardless of the consequences. He was willing to lay down his life for the Bible. He took seriously the exhortation of Charles Wesley: "Be a man of one book and let that book be the Bible!"

Dawson worshiped the Christ of the Bible, not the printed pages of the book itself. He had little time for those who preached sermons on the moral teachings and life of Christ but were soft and uncertain about whether the Bible is the Word of God. To say, "I love Jesus, but have my doubts about the Bible," was inconsistent as far as he was concerned.

Daws's position on the Bible had no elasticity to it. The Bible was the complete, written, infallible

Word of God. He believed in the verbal plenary inspiration of the Scriptures. Inerrancy had not become an issue in his day, but he certainly would have maintained that the Scriptures were without error of any kind. He came to his conclusion, however, not by a doctrinaire approach, but through the influence of the memorized Word of God on his life. One of his friends said with a slight smile, "Dawson knew what he believed and he could back it up with quotations from the Word. He was not terribly concerned with systematic theology, church methods, or techniques of evangelism . . . but on basic issues he was unpersuadable. The assurance of salvation, the development of newly born babes in Christ, the power of believing prayer, and the importance of being a disciple of Christ—these subjects were his meat and drink."

The Bible—not books about the Bible

As critics of his methods of using Scripture arose, Daws replied with a question that directed them right back to the critical importance of a thorough knowledge of Scripture: "Why was it not until three hundred and fifty years ago that God's people began to read and study the Holy Scriptures? They didn't have Bibles to read. Some couldn't read even if they wanted to. Often the organized church would not allow them to have a Bible. . . . It was easier to read books written about the Bible than it was to read the

Scriptures themselves. . . . If you're going to get back
to the Bible, you must get back to the Bible and not
books about the Bible. . . . I think that commentaries
or books about the Bible should be the little magnify-
ing glasses that say look again and see what you
missed in your primary study of the Bible. I like to tell
men about what I've read was the pattern for G.
Campbell Morgan, that great British pastor and
Bible scholar: 'Read the Bible and gain an outline;
meditate upon the Scripture at hand and gain an
analysis; sweat over the Word of God and gain an
understanding.'

   "I know men who can't even preach a message
unless they pull down books in the study. Let me give
you a tip on how to prepare a message from God.
Take the Bible, a pad of paper, a pencil, and get alone
with God. Then start praying and ask Him to pour
His message through you onto that pad of paper.
You'll soon find out if you are living up to the light
that God has already given to you.

   "Yes, I believe this is one of the weak spots of
our churches. Men study the subject very thoroughly, and they write the books, and then every-
body comes along and reads the books. The authors
know it, but the readers have never searched it out
for themselves.

   "That is largely where all these new Bibles are
coming from—the Scofield, the Thompson Chain
Reference, and the Analytical Bible. These study

Bibles are great, but they are a testimony to a great man who made a life study of the Scriptures. Their notes can be very powerful to you as you read and study them. . . . Make sure these notes are merely a help and not a crutch. They are not the Word of God—only the Bible is that!"

Often in staff retreats or Navigator conferences, Daws would share three basic principles of Bible study: first look for the primary interpretation, then search for secondary applications, and third, recognize that there may be a prophetic revelation. He had learned these principles from his own study as well as from Bible teachers he had known over the years.

Roy Robertson, Navigator evangelist and first Nav missionary to China, remembered being struck by Dawson's knowledge of Scripture the first time he heard him speak. "He was like a walking Bible to me. He had an uncanny ability to use the Bible. The way he could turn from page to page and come right up with the right verse was amazing. He was truly a craftsman of this trade. I compared him to one of the old prophets who would speak with power and dynamic force. Here was a man, made out of the common clay that I am made out of, who had contact with God. Yes, Daws was mighty in the Word of God."

Daws often phrased his ideas in epigrammatic statements. For example: "God says what He means and means what He says"—this was the way he laid out the doctrine of the authority of Scripture. "Predominant thought determines present action" would summarize the importance of meditation. "Emotion is no substitute for action, action is no substitute for production"—thus he pointed out the difference between pew-sitting and evangelism. Later he added the clause, "and production is no substitute for reproduction"—summarizing the difference between evangelism and disciple-making. He didn't use technical terms, but his convictions were plainly understood. He based his life and ministry on the *certainty* of the truth of God's Word.

Total commitment to the Word of God

Dawson's literal approach to the Bible placed on him the demand for literal obedience. This in turn meant personal discipline, which cost him considerable effort, since he had no special share of a disciplined life by nature.

Right up to the time of his death Daws demanded of himself total commitment to the Word of God, and he earnestly desired others to move "full steam ahead" with him. Dawson was especially rough on those men and women in church and organizational leadership. Luke 12:48 convinced him that these leaders, more than anyone else, had a commitment to a discipling ministry: "For unto whomsoever much is given, of him shall be much required. . . ."

Dawson was unusual in both his demands and his desire to get every Christian in the entire world to have the opportunity to dig into the rich treasure house of God's Word. Every facet of his life was permeated with the perfume of Scripture; the backbone of living the victorious Christian life was the Bible. His evangelism and follow-up of new converts was solidly based in Scripture, and his concept of multiplying laborers through personal ministry was the method the apostle Paul had used (see 2 Timothy 2:2). His vision of the church as a group of ministering disciples participating in body life was also scriptural (see Ephesians 4:11-12), and of course the fulfillment of the Great Commission (Matthew 28:19) was the key to his grand strategy.

*We started out on the
battleships of the United States
Navy, getting men to spend
time in the Bible. By the time
the war was over, we had
fellows on a thousand ships
and on scores of bases
throughout the world,
faithfully serving and witnessing for the Lord. I suppose there
was no greater secret than that
these men were in the Book and
the Book was in them. The
Word of God is the mighty
force within, that enables men
to do whatever it says.*

*I am absolutely convinced that
the Bible completely changes
the lives of men and women.
. . . It has completely changed
my life. I'll never be the same
again since I was introduced to
God's Holy Word, the Bible.*

DAWSON TROTMAN

Chapter 6
They All
Hold Swords

The Hand illustration was one result of Dawson's great drive to help others get a firsthand knowledge of the Scriptures. One of the verses he used in developing this tool was Song of Solomon 3:8: "They all hold swords, being expert in war: every man hath his sword upon his thigh because of fear in the night."

Daws's fertile imagination began to work on an image that would convey a spiritual truth. Since the

Bible is the "sword of the Lord," he reasoned, we need to grasp it with a spiritual hand. All five fingers of this hand play an important part in giving us a strong grip on the sword.

A means of grasping the sword

Roy Robertson remembered Dawson presenting the Hand illustration at Corpus Christi during the war years: "One evening he went to our Servicemen's Bible study and presented the illustration of the Hand. I'll never forget the way he presented it, using his own left hand, holding his little black Bible, as if it were a sword in the hand of a crusader for Christ.

"The four fingers on his left hand, as he explained to the thirty or so men present, were the four means of acquiring a grasp of biblical knowledge.

"The little finger represented the act of 'hearing the Word' preached or taught. Daws quoted passages from the Bible to remind us that *hearing* was basic to Christian growth. 'So then faith cometh by hearing, and hearing by the word of God'—Romans 10:17. . . . He quoted Jeremiah 22:29: 'O earth, earth, earth, *hear* the word of the Lord.'

"He then wiggled his ring finger and called that one 'reading the Word,' which he differentiated from studying.

"Then he drew attention to his middle finger and named that one 'studying the Word,' which involved research and writing things down. The study finger, he maintained, was the stabilizing finger on the hand. He then exhorted the servicemen not to study commentaries, expositions, lexicons, or concordances *first*, but to start with a firsthand study of the Scriptures themselves. Any workman who desires the approval of God, according to 2 Timothy 2:15, must be one who will study—dig, and dig some more.

"The index finger was Bible memory. 'Thy word have I hid in my heart . . .'—Psalm 119:11.

"At this point Daws would go back over the four fingers: Hearing, reading, studying, and memorizing. 'Each of these is not only recommended in the Bible, but each is also commanded.' The hand illustration left a great impression on his audience. A whole new way of being skillful in the Bible was presented.

"Dawson completed the story of the Hand with this warning: 'You will never grasp the sword without the thumb, which represents "meditation" on the Word. It is noticeable that three mighty men of God in the Bible—Joshua, David and Paul—were not only efficient in the art of waging a strong physical battle and hazarding their lives for the name of the Lord, but all of them knew that the real battles, the spiritual ones, demanded the weapon of the Word, the sword of the Spirit. Those three men all had plans to make sure their sword was sharp. Meditation sharpens the sword of the Word and keeps it sharp! The word *meditate* in its fullest sense suggests going over and over again the material to be learned so that the mind is filled with the facts. This is exactly what one does in reflecting on and applying memorized Bible material.'

" 'The thumb enables a warrior to use the other four fingers. When you fold your hand into a fist, notice how your thumb naturally moves over the top of the other four. So meditation conserves the fruit of the fingers—hearing, reading, studying and memorization—solidifying their strength and power. Just suppose that one or two or even three fingers of your spiritual hand are missing or that through non-use they atrophy; how effective will you be as a soldier of Jesus Christ?'"

The Hand illustration began with servicemen who needed to know how to handle their Bibles. Dawson's creativity supplied their need. He was by now constantly in search of new ideas or methods. Daily he asked God for new concepts on how to help people to know the Bible firsthand.

A quick way to find references
Another of his ingenious ideas was a tool that became a trademark of early Navigators around the world, a Bible index known as the Ladder. This device also grew out of Daws's efforts to guide his boys' class into the Word of God, specifically in helping them look up references. When he told his six

little fellows to turn to Romans 6:23, for example, one found it in ten seconds, another took twenty, another thirty, and a couple of the boys never did find it. By the time everyone had it, the boy who had found it in ten seconds was flipping rubber bands across the room because he was bored. Dawson tried another tack: "I decided the best way to handle the problem was to tell the class that from now on I would look up the verse and read it. But in my heart, I knew that wasn't the best thing to do. No, that might be a good thing to do, but not the best thing."

True to the pattern of his life, Dawson took his need to God in prayer: "Lord, I want to ask something of you. I know it's awful big. It's bigger than creating the world and holding the universe in space. But how in the world do you get a bunch of boys to find verses in the Bible without wasting lots of time?"

The answer came one day when Daws noticed a dirty streak across the edges of the pages of Psalms in his Bible. From then on, when he wanted to find Psalms, he looked for the dirty streak. It didn't take him long to broaden the application. "If I can do it with Psalms, I can do it with Isaiah. So I got a pen and put a thin line on my Bible where Isaiah might be found. Next thing I knew, I had one down for Matthew. Well, that was the answer, wasn't it? We just took the New Testaments of those little boys and put on them twenty-seven lines for the twenty-seven books and connected the lines together, making a ladder. Now it was fun finding the Bible references with the use of a ladder. In fact, Bible drills became a weekly project and never did one of my little experts take more than a couple seconds to turn to the exact page and verse."

Dawson encouraged his boys to carry their Testaments to school with them, but this caused some problems. When they tried to carry them in their shirt pockets, the Testaments kept falling out, and the other kids called them sissies. Daws wanted his gang to be regular fellows, so he told them to carry their Testaments in the hip pocket of their pants. But when the boys slid into home plate, that was the end of the Testament.

Daws found the answer in Velvet and Prince Albert tobacco cans. They were just the right size to carry a little New Testament and fit into the hip pocket. One of his boys felt he should get the tobacco smell out of his can; so he boiled it in lye. All the paint came off, and the can emerged bright and shiny, just like a chrome automobile bumper. Everyone wanted his to look like that. Soon, Daws had two or three boys in the business of selling chrome-looking cans for ten cents apiece to the other boys so they could carry their Testaments to school, as well as play ball. Now, when the boys started sliding into the bases, the Testament was safe while the pocket or seat of the pants was ruined. "But," Dawson reflected, "that isn't my problem."

These were some of the tools that sprang from Daws's vivid imagination. The Hand, the Ladder, the Topical Memory System, the organized ingenuity of the Navigator notebook—all were hallmarks of the early Navigators.

A working method for memorizing Scripture

Memorizing Scripture was very important to Daws as a method for making the Word a permanent and inherent part of his life. After he got started memorizing, he felt that others should naturally do the same. He described the development of his first memory system: "I worked feverishly to pick eighty-three key passages that every growing Christian needs. The first verse in the system was a favorite of mine: 'Now brethren, I commend you to God, and to the word of his grace, which is able to build you up . . .'—Acts 20:32. I put a little pledge card in with all the verses, which I totally expected everyone to sign immediately and return to me in Lomita. The pledge was something like this: 'Upon accepting these verses, I promise to fulfill the purpose for which they were designed. If at any time, I fail to keep this pledge, I promise to return them. . . .'"

Dawson told of the keen enthusiasm he felt as he produced this system: "Boy, this is surefire. I'll just get the folks who want it, and when I put the challenge out, they will write in and I'll send them the verses and the pledge. Boy oh boy, the sixty dollars to get them printed is the best money I have ever spent. . . . Those eighty-three verses were in a little book that would fit into your pocket or purse. There were five verses on a page with their references on the other side of the page. The printer liked them so well he printed up two thousand more than I had ordered and gave me one of the extra thousand. Between the two of us we got all three thousand of the booklets on memory.

"Several weeks went by, and I decided it was time to check up and see how some of the folks were doing. Those were the days when I was just beginning to learn about check-up and about people and their promises. I visited or contacted by phone a hundred people. Do you have any idea how many of those men and women got as far as a third of the way through the eighty-three verses?

"One person out of the one hundred. About ten of them had gotten through the first six or eight verses."

But Dawson wasn't easily discouraged. He was so convinced that Scripture memory was a basic need for Christians that he decided to keep trying until God had shown him a way to get people to do it. He knew that people needed motivation, help, and some kind of a system. But, he discovered, they also needed *someone* to be alongside and encourage them to press on.

To help him find some of the answers to these

needs, Dawson began to gather around him a group of men and women who were also biblically oriented. They began by asking such relevant questions as, Do we like to memorize Scripture? If not, why not? If we enjoy it, why is it so difficult to continue doing it? What are some of the reasons why church members in general are not familiar with the Bible?

"There were a lot of little things that hadn't yet clicked in our minds," Dawson later reflected. "First of all, most members in a local church don't realize the importance of the Bible. Secondly, they haven't made up their minds in a disciplined way that says, 'Hey, this Book is important—I'm going to conquer it.' Thirdly, and probably the most prominent, is that people never do get started. They are going to do it some day, but not today.

"The biggest waste of time is the waste of time in getting started. If folks do get started, they easily get sidetracked. This is one of Satan's greatest tools . . . the good is the enemy of the best. Most men that I know have been sidetracked from the time they were born—sidetracked on the things that take little drive and very little energy. I believe one reason that a lot of church members are washouts for the Lord Jesus Christ is the same reason they fail when they start to memorize Scripture passages—they get sidetracked.

"It's hard for the flesh to think God's thoughts. It's hard to concentrate on spiritual concepts. The brain doesn't like to think, especially if it is on spiritual matters. We like to sit down in a nice, soft chair in a cool breeze and float to heaven on a flowery bed of ease. I'm that way, and I know that in life, there are a lot of things that come easy, but getting the Word of God on your heart through memorization isn't one of them. It's spiritual. Anything spiritual is work, and my flesh and blood doesn't like work. But it *can* be done, and we can do it!"

The privilege of being thoroughly furnished
Every person, Dawson believed, could have the privilege of being "thoroughly furnished" for every good work. He would quote J.B. Phillips' paraphrase of 2 Timothy 3:17: "The scriptures are the comprehensive equipment of the man of God, and fit him fully for all branches of his work."

Dawson had an awesome respect for the power of the Word of God to change people's lives. He had seen young backcountry boys enlist in the military and, with the discipline of that regimented life and the influence of the Word of God, they would become men of God aboard their ships.

Dawson had seen milquetoast personalities transformed by the power of the Bible to become bold as lions in sharing their spiritual testimony. Under the authority of Scripture, men who had been enslaved to booze, gambling, and sex ended up back in civilian life as captains in industry or champions for Christ in the mission field. Of the first five sailors Dawson spent time with on the battleship *West Virginia*, four ended up on the foreign field as missionaries.

"Little is much when God is in it," Dawson firmly believed. Never is that expression more true than in the life of a man wholly committed to Christ and His Word. Here is the testimony of one such man—Les Spencer, whose request for help from Daws started a chain of ministry that became The Navigators: "In 1932 the Depression was very severe and, although we lived on a farm with plenty to eat, it was difficult for a family with six children to make ends meet. Since it was almost impossible for a young man just out of high school to find work in a small Illinois community, I decided to alleviate some of the financial pressure by joining the Navy. It wasn't long before Dawson Trotman entered my life, and we were off on an adventure, a spiritual adventure, that really has no ending. My life will never be the same again. Daws's love for God, for people, and for the Bible came through loud and clear to my young heart. His firsthand knowledge of the Word of God was something that I had never observed or seen in any other person. His skill in using the Bible was nothing less than awesome to me."

After his discharge from the Navy, Les had many years of fruitful and blessed ministry with the American Sunday School Union.

Many of the basic concepts that Dawson stressed were not new. People had been memorizing Scripture long before he was born, and the church had been practicing evangelism and Bible study and building converts up in the faith for hundreds of years. But Dawson was able to put all these together in fresh and appealing ways. Because he was an eclectic leader, Daws constantly gleaned the best from many sources. His drive and creativity enabled hundreds, and eventually thousands, of people to be "thoroughly furnished unto every good work."

One preacher observed, "Dawson was a driven man—driven by the Spirit of God through the Word of God to help every one of the children of God. Thank God, I'm one of those!"

A shoot-from-the-heart preacher

Dawson also believed that he was to "preach the Word of God urgently at all times, whenever you get the chance, in season and out, when it is convenient and when it is not" (2 Timothy 4:2, *The Living Bible*). To him this passage of Scripture meant, "Get into the Word, allow the Word to get into you, and get going and concentrate on getting the Word out to others."

Seldom did Daws preach or teach about *how* to memorize or study the Scriptures. He loved to preach the Word, and when he did, he moved listeners in the direction of memorization or study. "Out of the abundance of the heart the mouth speaketh" (Matthew 12:34). Because his well was full of the water of life, that water was constantly flowing forth. Dawson didn't do his preaching by standard homiletic principles. In his own "shoot from the heart" fashion, he would preach the Word as he saw it—provocative, dynamic, creative, life-giving, sin-abolishing, and essentially nourishing for every believer, young and old.

The following letter, from the pen of a young Presbyterian preacher, illustrates the remarkable effect that Daws's preaching could have on people: "My first acquaintance with Daws came as a result of the Billy Graham campaign in the city of Pittsburgh in 1952. I was just out of seminary, and one of my elders invited me to go to a follow-up meeting that was being conducted in the sanctuary of the First Presbyterian Church downtown. So at 6:45 on a Thursday morning I went down there, only to find the church packed with people listening to this man who had a strange-looking visual aid under his arm, which I later learned was his mechanical wheel to illustrate the full-orbed Christian life. I began to follow him wherever he went in the city. One morning I heard him three times before 10:00, and at the conclusion of that third meeting, I was impressed by the Spirit of God that here was a man speaking the Truth, and so I went to him and said, 'I'm a pastor of a small church and I need help.'

"He looked at me and said, 'How old are you,

Ken?' and I replied, 'Twenty-five.'

"'Great! We have been praying and asking God to raise up men your age who mean business for Him.'

"And I said, 'Mr. Trotman, I mean business!'

"I sensed in this man a heart to really know God and find out what God wanted him to do, and he had given his life to learn how to do it, and then was *doing* it. I hadn't met many men like that. I believe Dawson looked on the Word of God as being real communication from God, and he bent himself to obey that Scripture. Hence there was a power in his use of Scripture which was born out of obedience.

"Here was a man preaching with confidence and seeing people come to Christ, and I had that on my heart. Here was a man who not only was seeing people come to Christ for salvation, but who knew how to train them to reproduce spiritually, and that was tremendous to me as a pastor."

The spirit of the Lord God is upon me; because the Lord hath anointed me to preach good tidings unto the meek; he hath sent me to bind up the broken-hearted, to proclaim liberty to the captives, and the opening of the prison to them that are bound . . . To appoint unto them that mourn in Zion, to give unto them beauty for ashes, the oil of joy for mourning, the garment of praise for the spirit of heaviness, the planting of the Lord, that he might be glorified.

ISAIAH 61:1, 3

Chapter 7

Fisher of Men

The 1920s were boom years in the United States. In California, especially, the housing industry was running pellmell to keep ahead of the demands of families moving to the land of sunshine and oranges. In this business climate Dawson easily found a job at a lumber company in Lomita. The workers in the yards were rough and tough, and during the noon hour with their open lunch pails, they would gamble over a game of cards and share their filthy stories.

They loved to ridicule a lay preacher who came each week to share the good news of Jesus Christ. The preacher listened to their scoffing, but kept right on sharing the gospel.

Daws felt he should go up to this layman and introduce himself as a new Christian. But he also realized that if he did that, his buddies would identify him with the preacher. It was a small thing, but Daws struggled with it because he realized that God wanted him to "fly his colors" and to stand up and be counted for Him. But he was afraid. It took him two weeks to get up the nerve to shake hands with that preacher.

Dawson often met people in later years who would say to him, "Well, if I just had the strength and the drive and the initiative that you've got, I could be an outspoken Christian, too." Daws countered that type of thinking by saying, "You're looking at the most cowardly and weak Christian that ever lived. I had to pray every morning for two weeks for strength enough to walk up and shake that man's hand."

As time passed, Daws became convinced that God wanted him to stand up and share his testimony with his fellow workers at the main gate of the lumberyard. He kept telling God he'd do what He wanted him to do, but he continued to postpone it. "Lord, let me just live the life," he prayed. After three weeks of praying and misery he gave in and said "yes" to the Lord. That next week there appeared a notice on the bulletin board, just above the time-clock: PORKY TROTMAN TO PREACH AT THE MAIN GATE THIS COMING THURSDAY NOON! Although it later seemed like a small thing, obedience to God at that point was crucial. Said Daws, "If I hadn't made that decision, I think my whole Christian life would have been hurting."

Dawson did speak that Thursday noon at the main gate, and all the crew were there. He simply shared his testimony, telling of his run-in with the police, his vow to go to church the following Sunday night, and the contest that included memorizing Scriptures. Then Daws told those lumber workers the verses he had memorized. He shared all ten of them, with references! When he was through with his verses, he was through with his testimony. The lay preacher wrapped it up for that lunch hour.

Catching men alive
That was the beginning. Dawson spent the next thirty years sharing Christ with men and women all over the world.

But his witnessing began in his hometown of Lomita, California and in his everyday working world, the lumber company.

From his earliest days of walking with God, Dawson's main emphasis was on evangelism. His compassion for the lost grew greater as he grew older. He would try anything. At first he gave his testimony at the Fisherman's Club in Long Beach. That city had a famous amusement park called "The Pike," where sailors went for recreation. Here Dawson contacted hundreds of Navy men, and soon he was holding outdoor meetings in the band shell, where he and others would give witness to Christ through personal testimonies and preaching.

Dr. Charles Fuller broadcast his worldwide "Old Fashioned Revival Hour" from the Municipal Auditorium in Long Beach, and Dawson and his men quickly tied in with this strategic evangelistic outreach.

In June of 1940, he wrote, "The difference between catching men and catching fish is that you catch fish that are alive, and they die; you catch men that are dead and bring them to life."

During all these years of working for a living and yet giving forty to fifty hours a week to his outreach ministry, Daws never isolated himself from the secular world. The more he became involved with the church, following up new Christians, the more he spread out his tentacles to catch the non-Christian for Christ.

In those early days he devised a plan under which he wouldn't go to bed at night until he had witnessed to at least one unsaved person that day. On at least one occasion it cost him some sleep. "One night I went to bed about 11:30 p.m., and as I knelt down to pray, I remembered I hadn't talked to anyone about Christ. I said, 'Lord, I didn't talk to anybody today, but I'll talk to two tomorrow.' I got in bed, but I didn't sleep. 'If you let this go by tonight, Daws, you'll do it again and again,' says I to me. 'You give the devil an inch and he'll take a mile.'

"So I got up and dressed and started out in my car. I said, 'Lord, you gotta give me somebody tonight.'"

Daws saw a man running after a commuter train he had just missed, so he pulled up alongside and offered him a ride. The man accepted and asked Daws how far he was going. Daws replied, "I'm going exactly as far as you're going!" That answer scared the man, so Dawson got to the point quickly:

"Look, man, I'll get right down to business. I've been in bed already tonight. I want to get back. I just make it a rule in my life to tell the good, wonderful story about Christ at least once a day, and I didn't do it today. I got out of bed, and you're my chance. Can I start now so I can go home?" The man laughed and said, "You bet!"

In the following hour, Mr. Ford opened up his heart concerning his desire to know God, his attempts to go to church where the Bible was being shared, and his openness to the claims of Christ. In the wee hours of that morning, this businessman accepted Jesus Christ as his Savior, and Dawson was able to crawl back into bed a happy and sleepy fisher of men.

Dawson was a living testimony to his own slogan: "Every Christian a potential witness, every non-Christian a potential candidate for the Kingdom."

Dawson's commitment to evangelism can be summed up in one word: *love*. Dawson loved the Lord Jesus Christ; he loved the promises and commands of Scripture; he loved people. Out of this triple love came compassion, tenderness, and zeal. Dawson became Christ-centered. He tried to allow nothing to take away from God's glory. "My greatest goal in life is to glorify God."

Love for the common man

His primary concern in evangelism as well as in discipleship was with the individual, which some churchmen interpreted to mean he was "anti-organization," or critical of the church. He was constructively critical of the church's failures in some areas, especially her failure to follow up individuals and train them in discipleship, but he was never anti-church. He was a strong believer in the "priesthood of every believer"; he stressed both the privileges and the responsibilities of the individual believer priest.

People readily responded to the warm, personal interest Daws took in them. A sailor recalled, "I remember the first time I introduced myself to him. Daws turned to me and showed personal interest. Here I was, a lowly sailor. He didn't know me, but he took a very private concern. . . . He did this through a warm, friendly, and sincere interest.

"Dawson would often come to Oakland and, on more than one occasion, he would ask for me and invite me out to the lake for prayer. I just couldn't understand why Daws would ask for *me*, of all the dozens of men he knew in the Bay Area. He really felt that I could do more than I felt I could do. He had confidence in me, and he never talked down to me—and of course this would challenge me to do even a better job. Dawson expected more of me than I expected of myself, and that's one reason, no doubt, why I have done more than I would have done had I not met Daws."

Personal evangelism, Dawson felt, was the privilege and duty of every Christian, even the most ordinary. Special spiritual gifts for evangelism were not necessary. He often reminded his listeners of 1 Corinthians 1:26-29: "For ye see your calling, brethren, how that not many wise men after the flesh, not many mighty, not many noble, are called: But God hath chosen the foolish things . . . the weak things . . . base things . . . things which are despised . . . and things which are not, to bring to nought things that are: That no flesh should glory in his presence." With that verse as a backdrop, Daws would often say, "I'm not talking to you talented people; I'm just talking to the ordinary people. Frankly, I feel that the ordinary people are going to get this job done better than the talented people."

Dawson loved the common person in an uncommon way, perhaps because he felt that he too was cut from a very ordinary piece of cloth. His spirit of acceptance was refreshing.

Most Christians operate far below their capacity, especially in evangelism, Daws believed. To counter this tendency he encouraged people to think big, as this testimony from a friend of his reveals: "Daws really believed that I was important. He believed that I could do more, and he wanted me to do it. He set about helping me to get it done. In those early days of our relationship, he would blow my mind by painting big pictures of what I could do for God. It had the effect of making me reach a little bit higher and try to do a little bit better. Some of the reasons why, at sixty years old, I haven't quit and am still reaching for higher ground, and why I feel good and am encouraged with life as I am living it, are the things that Dawson Trotman imbedded into my life many years ago."

Matthew 4:19 gave the key, Dawson thought, to personal evangelism: "And [Jesus] saith unto them, Follow me, and I will make you fishers of men." He would break this down into the following three thoughts: "Go where the fish are, use the right equipment, and do your fishing with the right attitude and manner." The right attitude and manner could come only by obeying the command, "Follow me."

One of Daws's main avenues of evangelism was his home. He loved his wife, his children, and good homecooked food. But he also realized that their home, like their personal lives, was dedicated to God. Thus he was continually bringing men over for a meal. Sometimes Lila knew about it, and sometimes she was surprised, but she was never caught off guard. Daws told about their commitment to ministry in their home: "Early in our marriage, Lila and I claimed Isaiah 60:11 as the motto for our home: '. . . thy gates shall be open continually; they shall not be shut day nor night. . . .' We were married on Sunday, and we opened our home on Wednesday. We could only afford a two-day honeymoon. It was not long until the first sailor dedicated his life to the Lord. Men from every one of the forty-eight states have since learned about the Lord in our home. There was a period of six months when we seldom ate breakfast or our evening meal alone, because sailors were there. I believe with all my heart that one of the greatest soul-saving stations in the world is the home."

Scripture memory continued to bear fruit in evangelism. One evening, after the Trotmans had eaten dinner, everyone around the table shared a favorite Scripture verse that he had memorized, as was the tradition. A Navy man who had eaten with them was getting ready to give his only verse, John 3:16, when the Trotmans' four-year-old daughter

Ruth, sitting next to the sailor, began to recite her verse—John 3:16! There sat the sailor with his verse taken right out of his mouth by a little child.

Several weeks later Daws received a note from that same sailor, thanking him for the hospitality and then telling about going back to the ship that night with little Ruthie's recital of John 3:16 ringing in his ears. He suddenly realized for the first time that *he* was part of the "whosoever believeth in him should not perish, but have everlasting life," and that he had never accepted God's free love gift. Finally, in deep conviction of sin, he got down beside his bunk and gave his heart to Christ.

Handling fear in witnessing

Personal evangelism is often difficult. Telling others about a relationship with God through the Lord Jesus Christ requires a life of consistent prayer and time in the Scriptures. But even with all the protection and inspiration God gives, human fears and anxiety are forbidding. Daws experienced this fear, even in his mature Christian years: "Sometimes I am almost afraid to ask the Lord to give me a soul, because I know that if I ask Him, I am going to have to get busy. I have been a Christian for twenty-nine years, and it still frightens me to talk to a man about his need of salvation.

"Having that fear after so many years of doing personal work used to bother me. Suddenly I realized that such fear was only a little red light going on and off to remind me that it was 'not by might, nor by power, but by my Spirit, saith the Lord.' You never get to the place where you can do it on your own. You need Him."

Praying for witnessing opportunities can lead to unexpected experiences, such as this one that Daws found himself in one day: "I asked God's help in witnessing one day; then I began to look for a man. I was driving an old Model T at that time. . . . As I rode along, I saw a man hitchhiking on a highway in Los Angeles. I kept my eyes straight ahead and watched the red signal light at which I had to stop. Looking at this fellow out of the corner of my eye, I saw that he looked big and tough, so I decided that he was the wrong one. He wouldn't want to hear what I had in mind. As I waited for that red light to turn to green, it didn't change. It seemed like I sat there for thirty minutes. I thought the man had gone back to the curb, but when I looked at him, he was looking right at me. So I invited him in, and I lost no time in getting a gospel tract into his hand. He read it through and then handed it back to me.

"'What did you think of it?' I asked. He replied, 'I think it's wonderful.' I was startled at his answer and said, 'Oh, you're a Christian!'

"'No,' he answered, 'I'm not a Christian. I've been going to some tent meetings down this way every night for two weeks, and I can't get through. I have tried going down to the front every night, but I just can't seem to get through.'

"'Through what?' I asked.

"He answered, 'Isn't there something to get through?'

"I pulled over to the side of the highway, stopped, and turning to him I said, 'Buddy, I've got news for you. Somebody already got through.' All he needed was the simple gospel instead of being told to do something, and right there in the car he accepted Christ as his Savior.

"Do you know what I had been doing? I had been playing God. I saw this rough character, and I thought, 'He won't repent. He won't believe.' That was not my business. I have no right to decide for any other man whether or not he will accept the Lord. My business is to tell him the story and let him decide for himself."

One of Dawson's problems was in the "how to" of telling the story. He was so excited about it himself, he would often get carried away. This happened with his own father. He tried to lead his dad into a saving relationship with Christ but instead got him so upset that he said, "Listen, Daws, I'm in favor of your going into this yourself, but don't talk to me. When I'm ready for you to talk to me, I'll let you know."

Daws waited twenty-three years to talk again with his father about spiritual issues. Finally, at age seventy-seven, his dad came to the Lord.

"I might have won dad earlier," Daws reflected, "but I pestered him, and it drove him away. He told me the thing that caused him to come around was seeing the changed lives of the servicemen and what happened in my life. I was waiting to tell him the Good News and he was waiting for me to tell him. He had forgotten all about saying, 'When I'm ready, I'll tell you.'"

Immediately after his own conversion, Dawson threw himself into the young people's work at his church in Lomita and became an ardent witness for Christ. As he took young people to their homes after the meetings he would often speak personally to them about their relationship with Christ.

"Are you a Christian?" he asked a thirteen-year-old girl after a Sunday night meeting.

"I've gone to church all my life," was her confident answer.

"I didn't say, 'Are you a churchian?' but 'Are you a Christian?'"

"I've been baptized," was her reply, somewhat less confidently.

"But are you a Christian?" he pressed again.

He explained to her the gospel story and how she might receive Christ and have eternal life. Lila Clayton told him later that at 2:00 a.m., as she was still awake pondering the matter, she knelt beside her bed and asked Christ into her heart.

Young though she was, her life was transformed. She accepted the challenge to memorize Scripture and to establish a daily prayer life in fellowship with her Lord. She responded readily to the personal discipline of the Christian life which Dawson practiced and taught to others.

When at eighteen she became Dawson's wife, Lila's dedication to the Lord made her a fitting teammate for her husband. To both of them the Lord and His work were always first, their partner second by deliberate choice.

Daws believed that a Christian must always be reaching his neighbors, friends, and relatives. He had the rare privilege of leading his own wife to the Savior.

Graham Tinning shared his reflections on Dawson's evangelistic fervor: "Everywhere that Daws went he talked about Christ and what experiences he was having as a believer. He went from extreme disbelief to strong aggressive belief. Even in those days Daws was a dominant figure in any group. His language was not always the King's English, but everyone knew what Dawson thought and why."

No excuses

Dawson didn't have a great deal of patience with those people who had excuses for not sharing the goodness of the Lord: "People are always excusing themselves for not talking about Christ. They may say they don't have the strength or they aren't smart enough or they aren't talented. But God doesn't want Christians to do anything in their own weak way. 'I can do all things through Christ which strengtheneth me.'

"I have just returned from England recently where I spent some time with Stewart, a fellow who is both blind and crippled. He found the Lord through Billy Graham's Harringay Crusade. Do you know what he does? He gets on the subway train, and as he sits down, people help him because of his blindness and crippled condition. He hands them his Bible and asks,

"'Would you please read me the third chapter of John?' Or he pulls out his Scripture memory verse pack and asks: 'Will you review me on my verses?' God can use even the handicaps of one who is yielded to Him.

"Just relax. Don't try to cook yourself up a good deal. Don't do anything to get something for yourself. You let the Lord do that. Don't try to maneuver, don't use flattery. Don't do anything to attempt to get an edge. . . . Let the Lord do all the giving of profit. Why? The eternal God isn't shaken by our mistakes, sin or errors. He is not turned from His course by lack of materials, money or any other thing. He is watching over you day and night. He has your future at heart."

Daws was a perfectionist, and he demanded

thoroughness in those who worked with and for him. This trait was also true in his personal work. Sloppiness in presentation and shoddiness in materials were not acceptable.

Daws came down especially hard on young people who wanted to go overseas as missionaries but were not functioning as witnesses here at home. He found that most of them were neglecting the one condition Christ laid down as necessary to become a fisher of men: "Follow me."

For example, as a member of a mission board, he once spent five days interviewing candidates for overseas missionary service. He spent a half hour with each of the men and women, who had graduated from universities, colleges, and seminaries. He asked them about two main things: their devotional life, and evidence of abiding fruit in their ministries.

In answer to his first question, "How is your devotional life?" only one person out of twenty-nine interviewed said his devotional life was what the Lord wanted it to be.

When Daws asked why their quiet time wasn't up to par, there was a surprising similarity of answers. "Well, I'm attending this concentrated summer course and we're covering an entire year's work in twelve weeks, and the time pressure is just too much." Daws would say, "Let's back up to when you were in college—how was your time with God then?" He continued to probe backward into the lives of these men and women planning on a lifetime of service for God, and he found that never since they had come to know the Lord had they ever had a period of consistent victory in their devotional lives.

"That," said Dawson, "is one of the reasons for spiritual sterility: lack of communion with the living God."

The other question he asked was, "Do you know someone today, by name, who is living for Jesus Christ as a result of your ministry of winning and helping him in spiritual matters?" Dawson found that the majority had to admit that they were ready to cross an ocean, learn a foreign language, and attempt to do something in a strange culture that they had not yet accomplished right here at home.

Dawson believed that not just missionaries, but *all* God's people should be witnesses and spiritual parents.

*If you lead a person to Christ,
are you happy? Of course you
are. You're elated and so is
everyone else concerned—the
person himself and the angels of
God. But are you satisfied? No,
you shouldn't be. Jesus told us
to do more than just get converts. He told us to make
disciples. So you must stick
close to the person whom
you've led to Christ, and help
him grow till he takes his place
among those who can vigor-
ously and effectively advance
the cause of the Lord. When
that happens, he may be considered a mature, committed,
fruitful follower of Jesus Christ.*

LEROY EIMS

Chapter 8
The Apostle of Follow-up

Les Spencer was a young sailor in San Pedro, aboard the U.S.S. *West Virginia*. It was with this man that Dawson first started his lifelong campaign for multiplying disciples. Spencer told the story of his first meeting with Daws: "It was April of 1933 and I had just been assigned to the ship. Dawson sent a radiogram to me but it was received by another sailor with the last name of Spencer. I was in the midst of washing dishes when this man gave me the piece of paper.

"I took it, wet hands and all, opened it and read the message: 'Meet me at the San Pedro dock at 4:00 p.m. I will be wearing a dark coat, light trousers, and tan shoes. Dawson Trotman.'

"I was very puzzled and somewhat suspicious because I did not know anybody by the name of Trotman. I reasoned that somehow this must be some kind of a con game to separate a sailor from his money, so I promptly folded the message and put it in the pocket of my white jumper. The thought kept needling me all afternoon: How did Trotman know me? Where did he get my name? How did he know I was on the *West Virginia*? Curiosity got the better of me, so I arranged to have a buddy of mine serve the evening meal, secured a pass, and headed for the beach. I made sure to leave all my money aboard ship except for thirty-five cents for water taxi back to the ship later that night.

"I arrived on the dock just before 4:00 p.m. and began looking for a civilian who fit the description in the radiogram. Suddenly, out of the crowd of Navy men emerged a man walking at a lively clip who had a dark coat, light pants, and tan shoes. He stuck out a bony hand; a big smile broke across his face, and I received a hearty welcome from the man whom God had ordained was to play an important part in my life."

Dawson took Les home for one of Lila's famous fried chicken dinners, and then they drove up to the

Palos Verdes Hills, parked the car and began fellowshiping in the things of God. A security guard came up, saw the sailor, a civilian, and the Bible, and asked, "What are you men doing?" His job was to guard a nearby school building, so he had time to talk, and for about an hour Daws answered his questions about the Bible and explained the gospel to him.

On the way home, Les said, "You know, Daws, I would give my right arm if I could do what you did tonight."

Daws said: "Oh, no, you wouldn't."

"Yes I would," Les answered.

Daws pressed a little deeper to see if the sailor really meant it and said, "Oh, no you wouldn't, Les."

"I said I would!"

That determined tone of voice was what Dawson was waiting to hear. "Okay. It will not cost you your right arm, but it will cost you." For the next three months Dawson spent many hours a week sharing with Les from the Scriptures and from his own experience the things he knew about getting into the Word of God, evangelism, and follow-up.

At the end of three months, Les brought Gurney Harris over to the home and said to Dawson, "Give to this man what you have been giving to me. He can take it."

Dawson looked him in the eye and said, "No, I'm not going to."

Les was shocked and said, "I thought you wanted me to bring someone over who would be interested in going ahead in the Christian life."

Daws replied, "That's what I said, but *you're* going to give to this man what I've been giving to you."

Les answered, "But Daws, I've never been to Bible school, and besides, I don't know how to do it. I can't do it."

"If you can't give to Gurney what I've given to you," Daws said to Les, "then I have failed!" Les accepted the challenge, and being a man who really meant business, proceeded to teach Harris as he had been taught by Trotman, with occasional coaching from Daws when problems arose.

"If you can't do it . . . I have failed." In the years to come, Dawson often challenged his men with the words, "You're not going to park your babes on my doorstep." He was trying to awaken his spiritual offspring to their responsibility as parents in reproducing more spiritual offspring.

Like begets like

Daws's commitment to follow-up and multiplication developed through many years spent in trying to bring others to Christ. His methods sprang out of his experience: "It really wasn't till about 1940, even though I had been saved since 1926, that I realized that whatever I did, that's what my men would do regardless of how much talking I did.

"I began to see that the people that I was working with must lead their men and women to the Lord and then follow them up and get them into the Word like I was getting them into the Word. Like begets like!

"They were going through the stage that I was going through a few years before. I didn't have sufficient time with them and didn't have sufficient insight, and I didn't have sufficient foresight to see that I was going to have to take a long time to show them that they had a responsibility to their offspring. Because I didn't preach it by life and word, those that I was working with weren't doing it."

This realization struck Daws with startling force and clarity. He saw that following up his spiritual babes was his own great need. This was also the need of his men. And as he came to realize, *this was the need of the church*. Thus the conservation of spiritual fruit, following newborn Christians personally, became his consuming desire. Because he began to see that follow-up was the missing or weak link in Christian ministry, it was the link he constantly strengthened.

Speaking at a West Coast seminary in the mid 1950s, Dawson made this point to the young men: "Because there are missing links, do we throw the chain away? *No!* We're not trying to do that. We're just trying to put those links back in, because they are so important. And a chain is as strong as its weakest link. Follow-up of new Christians is one of the weakest links today in the church, in the Bible schools, and seminaries. I'm not saying they don't teach follow-up; in fact, they are trying to strengthen it. But we do feel that there's one link that's really weak, and that's the *one-on-one* principle."

As the years flew by, Daws became known as the apostle of follow-up. He was some twenty years ahead of his time in his discipleship thrust.

He was often misunderstood and criticized in those early days. It hurt him, but he felt that it was his responsibility to emphasize neglected truth, so he just kept strumming that one string—*follow up your spiritual babes, personally,* and teach your disciples to do the same and to teach theirs to do the same.

How did this man without much formal theological education get started with spiritual shepherding if it wasn't being taught, preached, practiced, or written about?

Daws told a seminary group about his personal pilgrimage into this new territory: "I had listened Sunday after Sunday to pastors' messages on a burden for souls. I read about it in books. Men and women that I respected in Christian leadership were soulwinners. So I started praying for a burden for souls. Within two weeks I had my first convert. Whether he was a convert to me or to the Lord, God only knows. He was a young Mexican boy hitchhiking his way home. I picked him up in my car that was running on just four cylinders and heating up terribly. I took this fellow some four miles out of my way to what was supposedly his home. I preached the Word to him. He believed. He said that now Jesus Christ was his Savior. As I started to leave, Juan said, 'Mr. Trotman, I want to go back to Wilmington with you.'

"'Why?' I asked. 'I brought you here to your home. I went way out of my way to do it.'

"Juan said to me, 'I came to rob my brother tonight. This is his home and he is on vacation with his family. But now I want to go to my own home.'

"It never entered my head that I had a responsibility to Juan. That was twenty-two years ago. Think what could have happened if I had imparted to Juan what I know today. Suppose I had stayed with him and helped him in the weeks and months following that car ride? Today Juan might be a missionary to his own country. I don't know where he is. I never even telephoned him and tried to contact him again. To me that is the great tragedy of today—we love to get decisions, converts, names and numbers. A tragedy. But I didn't know it then.

"In those early days there were lots of true converts to Jesus Christ, but not much emphasis on spiritual pediatrics. I remember somewhere around 1939, I was getting together with George. I remember saying one day, 'George, why aren't some of your babes growing? Show me the list of men on your ship that you are working with.' He pulled out his little notebook, and I said, 'Tell me about this one,' as I looked at a certain fellow's name on the page.

"'Well, Daws, when he accepted the Lord, I sure thought he had come through. He even had tears in his eyes. But Daws, he doesn't come around anymore—in fact, he avoids me on the ship now.'

"'Okay, George, but how about this one?'

"'I guess the same is true of him—neat guy, but I never see him.'

"We went down the list of names—nine of them. There wasn't one walking in the faith. Was it George's life? No! George lived a very solid life. Was it that George didn't know the Word? No! George lived a very consistent life of intake of Scripture. What was it? George was *so busy* winning the next fellow and using all his spare moments for the Bible study and heading for shore to attend some more meetings that *he didn't have time* to take that babe and stick with him through those early tough days of starting to grow in Christ. There weren't many 'fit ones' among the nine in George's notebook; they all had difficulty getting under way in their Christian experience.

"This experience with George, seeing the condition of his nine men, taught me a lesson: When Paul wrote Philippians 1:6, he was writing a follow-up

letter to the little band of believers at Philippi. Paul
followed them up by personal visits, with much
prayer, by making sure some of his godly friends
went by Philippi and paid a visit. Paul did it by many
lengthy and costly letters. He had no telephone, no
printing press, no typewriters, and no air transportation, but Paul got the job done. As you study the
Bible, you'll see how he had his converts in his heart,
day and night. *Daily* they were his concern."

New Testament pediatrics
Studying Paul's methods for following up his new
believers was a catalyst for Dawson's growing commitment to spending time and energy on helping
converts. He often reminded his disciples, "Effects
obey their causes by irresistible laws. When you sow
the seed of God's Word you will get results. Not
every heart will receive the Scriptures, but some will,
and the new birth will take place. When a soul is
born, give it the care that Paul gave new believers.
Paul believed in follow-up work. He was a busy
evangelist, but he took time to follow them up. The
New Testament is largely made up of the letters of
the apostle Paul which were follow-up letters to the
converts."

Daws marked 1 Thessalonians, the first New
Testament book written, with stars beside each
verse that said something from Paul's heart about
nurturing new Christians.

"I put twenty-four stars in this one little epistle. It indicates that at least twenty-four times Paul recognized his responsibility to follow up on the young church at Thessalonica. Why didn't I see this truth before?"

Following the example of the Bereans in Acts 17:11, who "received the word with all readiness of mind, and *searched the scriptures daily*," Dawson began to search the Scriptures on the subject of follow-up. He also got all those around him to do the same. They singled out the life of Christ in the four gospels for lengthy research. How did the Savior train His men? What went into those three years of earthly ministry? They concentrated on passages such as Mark 3:13-14: "And [Jesus] goeth up into a mountain, and calleth unto him whom he would: and they came unto him. And he ordained twelve, *that they should be with him*, and that he might send them forth to preach." What principles were involved in that phrase, "with him"?

They spent weeks of study in the book of Acts. Dawson saw that both Luke's gospel and the book of Acts were written because Dr. Luke wanted *one friend*, Theophilus, to get the straight story. It became clear that when *one man* becomes a true disciple, then another can become one, and then more, and then hundreds and then thousands—but it starts with one.

This kind of personal attention is important

because decisions are only the beginning—the birth of the Christian life. As Daws put it so often, "Making a decision is ten percent; following through is ninety percent." That follow-through, Daws believed, is done by people, not materials: "Is the answer merely materials to distribute to those who come to Christ? No, it is obvious from the experience of successful follow-up programs, both in the New Testament and out of it, that follow-up is done by *someone*, not by *something*. Paul wrote to the Romans, 'For I long to see you, that I may impart unto you some spiritual gift, to the end ye may be established.'

"After his extensive evangelistic journey in Asia, Paul was anxious to care for the new Christians: 'And some days after Paul said unto Barnabas, Let us go again and visit our brethren in every city where we have preached the word of the Lord, and see how they do'—Acts 15:36.

"Although he wrote to them, Paul considered *personal time* with them most necessary for effective building in their lives."

That kind of discipling takes time, energy, and money. To illustrate his point, Daws would remind his hearers that it takes nine months to bring a baby into the world, but to nurture, train, and prepare that child for life takes sixteen to twenty years. The apostle Paul took the time to nurture his spiritual children to maturity.

Turning to Acts 9:19, Dawson would note the phrases in that verse and in succeeding chapters that showed how much time Paul spent in follow-up work: "certain days . . . many days . . . a whole year . . . a long time . . . three Sabbath days . . . a year and six months . . . a good while . . . three months . . . two years." He would conclude with Acts 21:10: "we tarried there many days."

Daws's heart for evangelism was the catalyst for his emphasis on follow-up. "You can lead a soul to Christ in from twenty minutes to a couple of hours. But it takes from twenty weeks to a couple of years to get him on the road to maturity. But when you get yourself a man, you have doubled your ministry. That's why I so strongly believe that effective follow-up begins with effective evangelism. It includes providing conditions for a healthy spiritual birth, digestible food for the spiritual infant, and protection from spiritual disease, training and correction, encouragement and challenge, instruction and example. All these activities contribute to the goal expressed by Paul: 'So, naturally, we proclaim Christ! We warn everyone we meet, and we teach everyone we can, all that we know about him, so that we may bring every man up to his full maturity in Christ. This is what I am working and struggling at, with all the strength that God puts into me'— Colossians 1:28 and 29" (*Phillips*).

Daws was constantly experimenting with the

"how to" of spiritual parenting. One key principle he often preached, however, was strong personal commitment: "Let me share a couple thoughts on this follow-up principle. One thing for sure, you have to nurture them along. I don't know what you think that involves, but I know this: We find it takes a full six months of steady loving care.

"The main contact comes once a week or not less than every two weeks. It takes that much time to give them a good solid background—to get a few verses of Scripture in their hearts so that they can begin a new stand on many of the problems in life. They have to be shown how to take time to steady down into a regular devotional life with the Lord so that God can speak to them and so that they, in turn, can fully unload their hearts before Him.

"You'll remember that Christ gave his men three years. We do very well to get a man to do any kind of good work at all in six months. It sometimes takes two or three years before a babe in Christ is solid enough so that he can be given responsibility. We believe this thing works but we have to give it time.

"As I am talking with you, I know this: Unless follow-up is in your blood, it's going to take a long time to get it there. You can walk out of that door, saying, 'Daws, you're telling the truth and I'm all for you!' but that doesn't prove a thing. That won't produce results in your life. You're going to have to be sold on the things we are talking about so that they become a part of the fiber of your very thinking and a little bit more! You may not be able to get as many souls saved yourself as the great evangelists or those with Spirit-given gifts in evangelism, but you—and I don't care who you are—*you* can do follow-up. God has not called many to be talented, gifted, or brilliant personalities. In the main, God has chosen the ones that we in the church usually leave by the wayside through neglect."

Some of the "professionals" in evangelism were disturbed by Daws's philosophy on follow-up. But Daws, in turn, was disturbed by *their* priorities. "Why is it that organizations today can spend tens of thousands of dollars a year renting auditoriums, bringing in speakers, getting special music, and setting up a business office? Then they get a quality emcee, have some marvelous music, a solid message from the Bible, extend the altar call, and get the folks down to the front. Is all that money spent, and all those hours of energy exhausted, to say a few words of encouragement, a short prayer of commitment, shake some hands, say 'good night and God bless you,' and that's the end? How could men and women who know their Bibles do it that way?"

This kind of neglect, Daws felt, was occurring across the country and around the world. Jack Wyrtzen, founder of the New York-based organization Word of Life, shared how Daws helped him

overcome this problem in his evangelism ministry:
"On April 1, 1944, we had our first big rally in
Madison Square Garden with twenty thousand people inside and at least ten thousand out on the street
wanting to get inside. We were really riding high,
and as I look back we were kind of proud of the fact
that we had almost a thousand decisions for Christ.
Daws came in shortly after that to see us at our
Woodhaven offices, and he too rejoiced that Christ
was preached and that we had all those decisions.

"Then he clobbered me with, 'What are you doing for follow-up?' I asked him what he meant by
that. I told him we gave everyone a gospel of John,
had a prayer of commitment and said goodbye. I
don't think we even used decision cards back in those
days. Daws spent a lot of time with our whole staff
really impressing upon us the need of follow-up.

"The idea really came alive to us, so much so
that around 1948, after we had rallies in Boston
Garden, Yankee Stadium, and the Philadelphia
Convention Hall, we were really 'going bugs' on the
big job of following up thousands of young Christians."

During Navigator conferences, Daws would
hammer home the importance of follow-up in the
local church, warning his staff of the serious consequences of setting new Christians adrift to fend for
themselves. At one such conference he remarked,
"What God wants are men and women born into His

family who desire to be conformed to the image of His Son and to show forth the savor of His knowledge in every place. You lead a man to Christ. You tell him he's saved. You get him to join a church. You leave him. You let him go along living his former lifestyle. When does he do the most damage for God: before he met you, or afterwards? You know the answer. Preachers know it. Evangelists know it. And yet they go right on winning more souls and leaving them and winning more souls, and on and on it goes. Does it make sense?

"No; it doesn't make sense. You are in the greatest business on earth: that of bringing men and women into fellowship with Christ and to the place of greatest usefulness in God's marvelous plan. Your church is the heart and local headquarters of this tremendous program of taking the gospel of Christ to every creature and building in each believer a life that glorifies God. The worldwide success of this mission will be the giant reflection of its success in each community like yours."

Little did Dawson realize what God was preparing him for in the post World War II years. Many times he and Lila felt like voices crying in the wilderness—no one seemed to be listening. Most church leaders liked him, thought him a little strange and outspoken, and didn't fully comprehend what he was saying; but none could deny the results of his ministry. He was invited to denominational meetings to speak on the subject of follow-up, and many religious schools across America were anxious to have this dynamic speaker in their chapel services.

But few took it to heart. The traditional program must be kept rolling, and that took all the energy and money available.

The call to the Graham crusades

In 1950 Daws got a call from Billy Graham to help in city-wide crusade follow-up:

> Daws, we would like you to help with our follow-up. I've been studying the great evangelists and the great revivals, and I fail to see that there was much of a follow-up program. We need it. We are having an average of six thousand people come forward to decide for Christ in a month's campaign. I feel that with the work you have done, you could come in and help us.

This call had a great impact on The Navigators' work worldwide. Although some staff members thought this work would sidetrack The Navigators, it in fact anchored in Daws's heart the Scripture that God had been talking to him about, a promise in Isaiah 43:5-6: "I will bring thy seed from the east, and gather thee from the west; I will say to the north, Give up; and to the south, Keep not back: bring my sons from far, and my daughters from the ends of the earth."

At first, Daws protested that he had had little

experience with mass evangelism; his work had always been with individuals and small groups.

"Look, Daws," Billy answered, "everywhere I go I meet Navigators. I met them in school at Wheaton when I was a student there. I meet ex-servicemen all over the country who got down to business for God because of you and your men. There must be something to this."

Daws again felt he had to say no. "Billy, I wish I could, but I just don't have the time." But Billy persisted.

Daws *was* acutely aware that evangelistic campaigns were weak in follow-up. In fact, the whole church was. He also sensed that this Macedonian call to "Come over and help us" was not just from Billy Graham, but from God.

Billy, obviously annointed by God in evangelism, was going into the major cities of the world to assist the local churches in fulfilling the Great Commission. How could Daws refuse to strengthen this evangelistic thrust?

Daws later wrote to a friend about the turning point in his decision to accept Graham's proposal.

When Billy asked me to follow up for his campaign, I said to him, "Billy, you will have to get somebody else." That was the day before I left for Formosa.

He took me by the shoulders and said, "Who

else? Who is majoring in this? You are the only one I know who is majoring in follow-up."

I promised him, "While I am in the Orient I will pray about it." On the sands of a Formosan beach I paced up and down two or three hours a day praying, "Lord, how can I do this? I am not even getting the work done You have given me to do. How can I take six months of the year to give to Billy?" But God laid the added burden upon my heart.

In typical fashion, once Daws decided to tackle this job he did it with his whole heart. His staff supported him in the main, although some objected to what they called the "theology of mass evangelism" and quietly withdrew from the work. This quote from an article appearing in the Navigator monthly magazine *The Log* (1954) expresses Dawson's feelings about the joint effort with Billy Graham: "How thrilling to see thousands of folks deciding for Christ in a single crusade like Nashville or New Orleans. But even more thrilling to realize that each one of these is a precious life. Each one is important to our wonderful Lord.

"I often hear Billy say that though masses come together to hear the gospel, decisions for Christ are an individual matter. 'God so loved the world' . . . yet *every man* must face his personal hour of decision alone. . . .

"God is interested not only in your church, your mission group, or your young peoples' society. . . . He is interested in you. What is important to Him is your daily fellowship with Him in the Word and in prayer, your attitude of heart, your determination to live in unbroken victory. He is interested in your *personal* willingness to carry out His orders and to believe that He can be glorified through you."

While Dawson and his men were tending the thousands of inquirers from the Graham meetings each month, he never lost sight of his spiritual heart-beat, personal follow-up. In fact, personal follow-up was the focus of all his effort with the Graham Crusades.

The following excerpts from an article by Navigator staff member George Cripe (originally published as "Report from London," in *Brethren Missionary Herald*, Spring 1956) provides an example of how well Dawson's efforts in crusade follow-up worked. This account took place at Billy Graham's 1955 Wembley Stadium Crusade in London, where Dawson helped in the follow-up effort. Although The Navigators no longer do the follow-up for Billy Graham, the procedure today in the Graham Crusades is essentially the same as this article describes.

"It is 9:20 p.m., May 14, 1955. Nearly one hundred thousand rain-drenched spectators in London's Wembley Stadium are hushed in awed silence as Billy

Graham's final words of invitation echo throughout the Stadium. Rain, which has been falling softly throughout the service, suddenly begins to pour in diagonal sheets which glitter in the bright floodlights and drench the emerald turf. As Billy stands with head bowed and the choir sings softly, 'Just as I Am,' a trickle of humanity begins to seep down out of the packed stands, in moments swelling to a mighty torrent of 3,400 people who pour down onto the field.

"High in the stands on this fateful night sits a man who has wandered into Wembley stadium out of curiosity. Often he has come here to watch the dog races. Tonight, as he listens to the Gospel message, an unaccountable yearning grips him. As Billy gives the invitation Tom Edmonds gets up out of his seat and walks down onto the cinder track into the lashing rain and the blinding glare of huge floodlights. As he joins the swelling crowd in front of the speakers' platform, he suddenly realizes that someone is speaking to him. 'I say, would you care to share this umbrella with me, friend?' It is the man next to him. Gratefully Tom moves under this partial shelter.

"Standing there in the rain and glare, Tom's mind searches for the reason he came forward. 'I don't have the answer,' he thinks. 'Nothing's changed yet.' He listens as Billy Graham instructs the converts. He repeats the prayer of confession. Still the hunger in his heart is unsatisfied. 'If I could only talk to Billy personally about my problem,' he conjectures.

"With a start Tom realizes that the man with the umbrella is speaking to him again. 'My name is Edgar Mendenhall,' the man announces. 'I'm a counsellor in the Crusade, and I'm wondering if I might be of any help to you. Perhaps you'd care to tell me why you've come forward.'

"'Edmonds,' responds Tom. 'I'm afraid I'm really confused. You see, I don't really know *why* I've come forward, except that—it seemed I had to, somehow. My life's not been what it should be. Not bad, really; just aimless. And of a sudden, tonight, it seemed terribly empty. When Mr. Graham spoke of having peace with God, I realized that I wanted that peace more than anything else in the world. I'm afraid I don't have it, though, even now, after having come all this way down here,' he ends rather lamely.

"'But you can have it, you know,' replies the big man. 'Here, hold the umbrella for a moment, will you?' Edgar Mendenhall draws a plastic covered Bible from his coat pocket. 'You see, in the first place, you need to settle everything on God's Word. Heaven and earth will pass away, but God's Word shall never pass away. So everything I tell you tonight will be based on the Bible. You will accept that, won't you?'

"'Oh yes, of course,' replies Tom.

"'Then there *is* an answer to your problem.

Now the first thing you need to know is that God will receive you, if you sincerely come to Him. He says, "He that cometh to me, I will in no wise cast out." He will receive you, if you have come in *real sincerity*.'

"'As far as I know, I have.'

"Edgar Mendenhall turns quickly to key Scripture passages. Romans 3:23—'All have sinned . . .' Romans 6:23—'The wages of sin is death . . .' Romans 5:8—'Christ died for us . . .' John 1:12—'But as many as received him, to them gave he power to become the sons of God. . . .' He asks Tom to read the verses aloud, making sure that Tom understands each passage before turning to the next one.

"As he ponders these Scriptures, the light of a great truth breaks over Tom's face. 'God loves me. My sins are washed away. I become a child of God— He's offering me eternal life!'

"'Will you accept this gift?'

"'Will I?" says Tom. 'Will I? Of course I will.' In his excitement he has lost his English reserve. They both bow their heads, and, as the rain drums steadily on their umbrella overhead, Tom finds peace with God through Christ.

"Edgar Mendenhall now makes certain that Tom is trusting the Scriptures alone, and not his feelings, for salvation. He gives Tom a booklet called 'Beginning with Christ' with four verses on 'Assurance of Salvation' and encourages him to memorize 1 John 5:11-12 before going to bed. Edgar stresses the importance of church attendance, private prayer, and witnessing. To encourage him, he introduces Tom to a man whose lapel bears a large ribbon labeled ADVISOR. To this more experienced Christian worker Tom gives his first testimony of conversion. 'I surely appreciate the help that other minister gave me,' says Tom at the end of his interview with the Advisor. 'Oh, didn't he tell you?' says the Advisor. 'He's not a minister. He's an interior decorator.'

"Tom walks by other umbrella altars where seeker and counsellor are still in earnest conversation over an open Bible. The rain is beginning to subside as he leaves the Stadium, and in his heart there is a great peace.

"As soon as Tom leaves, the follow-up office in the east wing of Wembley Stadium swings into action as volunteer workers process thousands of decision cards.

"The following afternoon Tom receives a personal letter from Billy Graham, congratulating him on his decision and offering several helpful suggestions on how to live the Christian life. Special emphasis is laid on the speedy memorization of the four 'assurance' verses, so that he may be equipped with the sword of the Spirit to ward off the initial assaults of the devil. The letter also encourages him to read the Bible daily, begin to pray daily, and go to church.

"Within forty-eight hours the counsellor who led him to Christ calls and gives him a personal word of encouragement. And before the week is out, the pastor of the local church visits him, offers further instruction, and extends a warm invitation to attend services.

"The crusade follow-up does not stop here. Tom will receive an invitation to a special converts' rally and at least one more letter from the follow-up office, enclosing the first lesson of the Navigators' *Introductory Bible Study*. The counsellor will call at least once more to see how Tom is coming along.

"The heart of this synchronized personal counselling and follow-up program—apart from the highly technical office organization—is a six-week, pre-campaign training class for personal counsellors. This concentrated course in personal evangelism is taught by the Reverend Lorne Sanny, vice president of the Navigators and director of follow-up for the Billy Graham team. It covers topics ranging from the personal devotional life through Scripture texts dealing with specific spiritual problems. These principles will become a vital part of the counsellor's personal life.

"The counsellor also is taught how to win a person's confidence, how to discern his *real* needs—as distinguished from the first one he may mention—and how to meet that need from God's Word. He is taught how to lead a person to make an intelligent decision and how to follow through afterward in helping him grow in prayer, the Word, and witnessing.

"Along with an identifying badge, each counsellor receives special written instruction outlining the procedure to follow in the crusade meetings. Each night he is assigned to a special counsellor's seat reserved for him in the main auditorium. During the invitation he falls in step beside a person of his own age and sex who is going forward, or if unable to do this, he proceeds to the counselling area and awaits an assignment from an Advisor. The counsellor's final responsibility, after praying with the seeker, is to introduce him to an Advisor, who solicits the convert's testimony and clears up any remaining problems.

"The architect of this comprehensive and closely knit follow-up structure is forty-eight year-old Dawson Trotman, founder and for twenty-three years president of The Navigators. His hustling Christian organization is dedicated to the proposition that every newborn babe in Christ has a right to grow up into maturity and become a fruit-bearing Christian. They feel that without a spiritual 'parent' who will give individual care and attention a new Christian may become permanently stunted, even if he has had a genuine rebirth. Asked by Billy Graham in 1950 to become team follow-up director, Trotman brought to bear on the mass evangelism situation all of his years of experience in personal work and individual follow-up. The result has been a meshing of the two into the highly synchronized movement of the present-day Billy Graham follow-up program. Although forced to devote most of his time these days to the world-wide demands of his expanding missionary organization, Trotman maintains an active interest in Graham team follow-up through Navigator Vice President, Lorne Sanny, who has assumed virtually full responsibility for the follow-up program. When Billy Graham conducted meetings in Europe and Asia, local Navigator representatives handled the follow-up in a manner similar to the London Crusade.

"Perhaps the most beneficial aspect of this whole follow-up program is that it puts large numbers of laymen to work winning souls. Many date the beginning of their spiritual growth from the night when they led their first soul to Christ in a crusade counselling room.

"Edgar Mendenhall and his wife, for example, who were converted shortly before Billy's 1954 London crusade, felt they were too spiritually weak to counsel others. 'We need help ourselves!' they argued. Nevertheless, they attended the counsellor training classes, and during the 1954 London Crusade they personally counselled 114 people, sometimes staying up until 2:00 a.m. to follow up their converts.

"A year later they can account for 110 of these original 114 growing in grace and established in a church! During Wembley in 1955, Tom Edmonds was only one of many this man and his wife led to Christ.

"This follow-up system in no way substitutes for the local church's responsibility. The aim of the program is that every seeker makes an intelligent decision, gets an extra boost during the first forty-eight hours, and gets linked with a good local church. Simple Bible study helps are sent to him for a short time from the Crusade office, but from here on the job of following him up is largely up to a local church.

"Since it is often physically impossible for a minister to give personal care to all of the new converts sent his way, one phase of the crusade follow-up is setting up a follow-up team of laymen within the local church, coached by the pastor. Each team member adopts several of the newcomers and meets with each one regularly until the convert is established in a Christian walk. Any problems are brought up and prayed over at the weekly get-together of pastor and team member. Where adopted, this plan has proven highly successful.

"Lorne Sanny is a man with an eye for efficiency and a heart as big as the whole wide world. The counsellor instruction material is one of his distinctive contributions to the crusade follow-up, but he is also an indefatigable streamliner. 'We are never satisfied with our achievements,' he says. 'After each crusade, we see things that need to be improved.'

His tried and true procedures are the results of this drive for improvement.

"Today, Tom Edmonds is a sparkling Christian witness in his English community. He has won several of his friends to Christ, and one of these has won his first soul to the Lord. Tom isn't aware of all the effort that goes into the intricate follow-up program that helped him get a start in life, but he is very aware of this one thing: 'Once I was blind; but now I see.'"

As Dawson became more and more involved with Billy Graham, more of his team became involved also. When he went to be with the Lord in 1956, almost all of the key leadership of The Navigators were in some way tied in with the Crusade work. And this was the way he wanted it! "Anything worth doing, is worth doing with all your heart, with all your men, and with all your pocketbook."

From follow-up to discipleship

As Dawson continued his work with the Graham Crusades and within his own organization, his eyes were gradually but surely being opened to a biblical truth that went beyond mere follow-up: that of discipleship—mature Christians winning and training others to win and train others. In other words, spiritual reproduction. This privilege, he believed, was the potential of *every* Christian. "A reproducing Christian doesn't have to be an orator, and he doesn't have to have a stimulating personality. He doesn't have to be beautiful or have an outstanding education. In the physical as well as the spiritual realm, every person who is healthy, fairly mature, and not sterile, can be a parent to children. I believe it's time that all the children of God, each one of them, began to think of himself as a *producer* and to think of those he reaches for Christ as *reproducers*. Don't be satisfied until you see your grandchildren in the Lord and then, in time, some great grandchildren. *There's a goal for you!* There's something to keep you on your knees in prayer and searching the Scriptures for more of the milk of the Word."

Physical multiplication began as a command from God, recorded in Genesis: "Be fruitful, and multiply, and replenish the earth . . ." (1:28). Dawson believed that this command for physical reproduction was an analogy to God's plan for spiritual reproduction. To emphasize the importance of one human being in the reproduction process, Daws brought up Isaac's brush with death on Mount Moriah. Here was one man whose death could have cut off the proliferation of an entire race. "Imagine if Hitler had been present on Mount Moriah," Daws speculated, referring to the man who had made it his lifelong goal to exterminate Isaac's race. "If Hitler had caused Isaac's death, when Abraham's knife was poised, he could have killed *every Jew* in that one stroke. I believe that is why

Satan puts all his efforts into getting the Christian busy, busy, busy, but not producing."

Daws used this powerful illustration to convict his listeners of the crucial necessity of investing their time and energy in the lives of others, and not wasting it in unproductive activities. He began to really bear down on the matter of personal discipling—zeroing in on spending time helping at least one person. "Men, where is your man? Women, where is your woman? Where is the one whom you led to Christ and who is now going on with Him? The curse of today is that we are too busy. I am not talking about being busy earning money to buy food. I am talking about being busy doing Christian things. We have spiritual activity with little productivity. And productivity comes as a result of what we call follow-up."

Follow-up should result in reproduction, and then multiplication of reproducers. Dawson's favorite illustration of this truth is found in 2 Timothy 2:2. "And the things that thou has heard of me among many witnesses, the same commit thou to *faithful men*, who shall be able to teach others also." Here in this verse are four generations of spiritual heritage: Paul, Timothy, faithful men, and others. What Timothy was learning from his adoptive father he was to transmit to faithful men who, in turn, would teach others to do the same. This process is reproduction.

The primary aim of Dawson Trotman, and that of The Navigators to this day, is, "To know Christ and to make Him known."

*Whatever you have learned or
received or heard from me, or
seen in me—put it into practice.*

PHILIPPIANS 4:9 (NIV)

*The one indelible impression I
have of him is that he was a
pacesetter.*

JIM DOWNING

Chapter 9
Leading the Way

One reason that Dawson Trotman was so persuasive in both his personality and his preaching was that he practiced in his day-to-day life what he was proclaiming to others. He *lived* what he believed and taught. He called this principle "pacesetting."

If you don't have it, don't preach it
Daws didn't see many pacesetters in the church of those early days. Being an example to believers

seemed to be a lost art. He used to insist that it was necessary to do something *yourself* in order to get somebody else to want to do it. People generally didn't seem to think the victorious Christian life was possible because they didn't see it in their leaders. Daws put his faith into action first—then taught others what he had learned. He memorized Scripture long before he attempted to get others to hide God's Word in their hearts. He was himself sharing Christ with others before he started enlisting Navy men to be "ambassadors for Christ."

"If you aren't setting the pace, then you have no life to pass on except that which is your own weak and ineffective experience." Daws had a favorite expression: "Don't talk an inch beyond your experience. If you don't have it, don't preach it. If you're not practicing it in your own life, don't talk about it to others." This basic principle of pacesetting in part explains the success of Daws's ministry.

One of the men closest to Dawson throughout his entire adult life was Jim Downing. Observing Daws by living with him, ministering with him, and serving with him in the Navigator organization elicited this observation from Jim: "The indelible impression that I have of him was that he was a pacesetter. He knew what should be done, he did it, and he never asked anybody else to do anything that he had not done himself. This particular quality would make him a success no matter what he went into. His energy, his drive, his intelligence, and zest for life . . . coupled with his intense desire to 'lead the pack' . . . made him successful in the one great job he undertook."

Dawson's account of Vic McAnney, a sailor aboard the U.S.S. *Astoria*, illustrates the power of pacesetting in witnessing: "Vic was a sweet guy. Now you don't use that term often in connection with a 'man's man,' but once in a while you can do it in a complimentary way; and Vic was, indeed, a sweet Christian sailor. We often refer to him as a 'first-class baker and a first-class Christian.'

"Since he was a boss in the kitchen aboard ship, Vic didn't have to mix dough or wash the pots and pans. The *Astoria* was going across the equator one time, and it was hot . . . and down in the bake shop in the hold of that ship, it was really hot. Vic was down there putting pies in the oven and sipping iced tea. He remarked to one of his men: 'Boy, if it wasn't for this iced tea, I couldn't keep going.' This fellow knew Vic real well, and although he had not trusted Christ as his Savior yet, this man had sensed Christ's reality in the seaman first-class, and said, 'Mac, you've got something bigger than that iced tea to keep you going.'

"Often under the South Pacific stars, Vic would lead a Bible study on deck beneath one of the eight-inch gun turrets. Before the *Astoria* sank off the Solomon Islands, Vic had led forty of her crew to

Christ, and, as with most men, they 'would rather see a sermon than hear one any day.'"

These Christian military men tried to do their work aboard ship not just adequately, but excellently. Through their workmanship, they demonstrated the power of Christ in their lives.

Follow the leader

One day in the spring of 1954, during a flight from southern California to the Bay area for a conference at Mt. Hermon, Dawson began discussing his evening message with me. The text was Proverbs 23:26. "My son, give me thine heart, and let thine eyes observe my ways." He wanted me to think out loud with him about some examples in the Bible in which people learned by seeing, not just by hearing. We mentioned some of the military leaders like Moses, Joshua, and David who led their men into battle. They set the pace by being out in front. Suddenly Daws said, "Hey, Bob, how about the farm boy, Gideon? Remember how he went into battle formation with a mere three hundred men against a mighty force that was camped in the valley 'like grasshoppers for multitude; and their camels were without number, as the sand by the sea side for multitude'?"

Daws got his Bible out of his little brown carrying-case and opened it to Judges 7:17. As if he were reading it for the first time, he shared with me: "And [Gideon] said unto [his men], 'Look on me, and *do likewise*. . . . It shall be that, as *I* do, so shall *ye* do. When I blow with a trumpet . . . then blow ye the trumpets also. . . ." I have never seen anyone more excited about anything than Daws was by that passage. He was so charged up that if that plane we were on had landed in Bakersfield, he probably would have flown on up to Santa Cruz on his own. "As I do, so shall ye do."

The idea that gripped Dawson's mind that Friday was this: A son will observe and imitate his father's ways. Solomon said it, Gideon said it, but who was saying it now? That evening Dawson spoke to an eager audience of five hundred conferees. He started with some Trotman humor, gave them a few war stories, and then got into his message—"Pacesetting."

"Have you ever watched a flock of sheep?" Daws asked the audience. "If you get that chance, take it. Sit and observe. One lamb will jump over a couple of boards. Then another will follow, and then another. The shepherd pulls the boards away and what happens? The lambs continue to jump over where the boards used to be. 'Follow the leader' is the game they are playing. Habit says to them, 'Jump,' even though there is no reason for jumping any longer."

Daws went on to graphically describe how people are like sheep, playing games, with someone out in front leading the way. "You can't get others to do what you aren't doing yourself. If you don't jump, don't expect them to jump. You can't give something away if it isn't yours."

Then for the next hour, Dawson took those five hundred people through the New Testament, and showed them what Jesus, the disciples, and Paul had to say on this vital principle of Christian living. "Jesus didn't say to His men here by the seaside of Galilee, '*Listen* to me and I will make you fishers of men.' Nor did He say to those hearty men, '*Read some of the books on the subject*, and that will make you fishers of men.' No, Jesus said to them, '*Follow* me.' And for the next three years they did just that. Seldom did Jesus teach with mere words, but He taught by demonstration, illustrations, and living out His own life before them. In The Navigators, we call this the 'with Him' principle. It is based on the whole context of the gospels, but particularly on verses like Mark 3:14—'He ordained twelve, that they should *be with Him*, and that He might send them forth to preach.'"

As the Mt. Hermon crowd was busy taking notes, Daws turned with them to the book of 1 Corinthians. He loved to pitch his spiritual tent on the fourth chapter, verses 14-16: "... my beloved sons ... though ye have ten thousand instructors in Christ, yet have ye not many fathers ... I have begotten you ... be ye followers of me." Then quickly he would turn to 11:1—"Be ye followers of me, even as I also am of Christ."

His speaking tactics were often unorthodox, and this evening was no exception. Seeing that his audience was getting tired, Dawson decided to illustrate his point physically to wake them up. He went out into the audience, selected two young fellows, and got in line with them. "Right foot forward! Left foot forward!" Those three men, as close together as possible, marched across the front of the Tabernacle building as one. At the middle, in front of the pulpit, he made them stop. "Let's call the first one in line Jesus Christ. You are the leader and we are followers.

"You in the middle, your name is Paul. Just like the man who wrote the letter to Corinth and the little church there. My name will be Crispus. My home is Corinth. Lived there all my life. Paul came in and preached in Corinth, I listened to all that he had to say, and I became a believer of the Lord Jesus Christ.

"I, Crispus, am walking in the footsteps of Paul. Paul, you walk as closely as you can to Jesus. Get in step with Him. If you are following in His footsteps and I am walking in your footsteps, then I am walking in the footsteps of my Lord.

"If we are all in step, and Paul is keeping low and out of sight, when I look at him, I don't see Paul. He is so close to Jesus Christ, that all I see is Christ.

"That's pacesetting. That is the biblical pattern. This is what Paul was also telling the church at Philippi: 'Those things, which ye have both learned, and received, and heard, and seen in me, do: and the God of peace shall be with you'—Philippians 4:9."

Dawson had the young men look up these passages of Scripture, which he felt were important illustrations of or commands to be pacesetters: "Brethren, *be followers together of me*, and mark them which walk so as *ye have us for an example*" (Philippians 3:17); "And *ye became followers of us*, and of the Lord, having received the word in much affliction, with joy of the Holy Ghost" (1 Thessalonians 1:6); "Let no man despise thy youth; but *be thou an example of the believers*, in word, in conversation, in charity, in spirit, in faith, in purity" (1 Timothy 4:12).

After relating several stories from his own life on mistakes he had made and lessons learned in pacesetting, he concluded, "I must be living the Christ-centered, Spirit-filled life if I would have another whom I am working with live that kind of life. I must be in the Word of God on a daily basis, if I would have my man be a man of the Word. I must be a fisher of men, if I want my spiritual Timothy to reproduce after his kind. . . . As Paul says in 2 Thessalonians 3:7 and 9—'For yourselves know how ye ought to *follow us*: for we behaved not ourselves disorderly among you . . . to make ourselves an example unto you to follow us.'"

That spring day at Mt. Hermon in 1954 was one of the few occasions when Dawson devoted an entire message to this subject. He felt much more comfortable practicing it than preaching it. If he saw a weak link in the chain of Christianity he would try to set the pace in that weak area, speak out in a positive manner, and hope that others would pick up the message they heard and observed.

Another story from Dawson's life dramatizes how he set the pace by putting his convictions into practice. A young pastor wrote, "Dawson spoke at our denominational family conference in the summer of '54. I had the opportunity of driving him to his plane following the last service. He had met with men early in the morning, and so as we were riding along in the car he got very sleepy. I had many things I wanted to talk to him about, and suddenly he said to me, 'Ken, would you mind if I slept for a little while?' And so I told a fib. 'No, Daws, I don't mind at all. Go right ahead and sleep. We're about an hour from the airport.'

"Of course, I was very disappointed down inside, for now I wasn't going to have the chance to talk with him. We drove on in silence as he slept, and sure enough, he only woke up as we drove into the parking lot of the Des Moines airport. As we parked the car and were unloading his bags from the trunk, he looked at his watch and said, 'Now this is great. We're checking in at least an hour ahead of time, so we've got some good time for you to share what's on your heart.'

"After taking care of the travel details, we went over to the lounge and he remarked, 'Let me give you a little principle, Ken, that might help you in the ministry in years to come. Never give counsel to a man when you're sleepy. I know you had some things you wanted to talk about, and I wanted to talk with you. But I also knew that if I would sleep, I would get refreshed, and then I'd be at my best to talk to you. So let's talk!' That incident has never left my mind. Dawson taught me by example more than by words. We did have a great time together, but he wanted to be at his best so his counsel would not be 'tired out and sleepy,' and so he was willing to be real with me. It reminds me of Proverbs 27:17—'Iron sharpeneth iron; so a man sharpeneth the countenance of his friends.'"

Dawson had the same desire to see the young men and women of the Navigator staff setting a spiritual pace that Paul had for his young recruit, Timothy. "Be thou an example of the believers" (1 Timothy 4:12). Timothy, in charge of the church at Ephesus, had been called upon to give utterance to the lofty precepts of the gospel and the Christian life. Much of his teaching would come into violent collision with the natural desires of those to whom he ministered. It was of the utmost importance that his own life should exemplify the teaching set forth, otherwise his relative youthfulness (he was in his thirties) could become an occasion of offense. Paul instructed Timothy to be an example for the believers "in word, in conversation, in charity, in spirit, in faith, in purity." Timothy had to set an example in his private life (even in his thought life), as well as in his public ministry and social relationships.

This pacesetting principle was observed in Dawson's life by Doug Sparks, an early overseas Navigator representative. He told about a vivid demonstration of modeling after the Master: "I was in the mountains of Taiwan with a Taiwanese leader, Pastor Lo, who was working among the Ami tribe. On one of Dawson's Oriental trips, he had taught in a local Bible school and had also spent several days visiting the mountain people, some of whom were former headhunters but now were believers in the Lord Jesus Christ. I asked Pastor Lo what he thought about Dawson Trotman and what stood out in his mind about Daws. I was expecting some great spiritual truth or that the godly Chinese man would share some dynamic thing that had happened as the two men were together.

"Pastor Lo just turned to me and, smiling, said, 'Mr. Trotman is the most incredible foreigner that I have ever met. One day we walked through a steady rain to several outlying villages and ministered the Word of God. Returning home late in the afternoon, wet, cold, our shoes covered with mud, we both agreed that a cup of hot tea would be just right. As is our custom, we both removed our dirty shoes at the

entrance, and I went on into the kitchen to prepare a
little refreshment. When I returned in about fifteen
minutes, there he was on the floor with a small stick,
a piece of cloth and water, and would you believe it,
he had shined my shoes! An American cleaning the
shoes of me, a Chinese.'

"Yes, I believe it, for that was just the way
Dawson was. If he saw that somebody had a need, or
if there was something he could do to help another
person or organization, he was thrilled to do it. He
was always looking for opportunities to be a friend,
an influencer, a counsellor and a great encouragement. 'Be thou an example.'"

An amusing story from the late 1940s illustrates
how other Christian leaders reacted to Daws's challenge to pacesetting. At a dinner meeting for the
leaders of Youth for Christ, at the home of Daws and
Lila Trotman in South Pasadena, California, the
guest list included Billy Graham and Cliff Barrows;
Torrey Johnson, president of Youth for Christ International; Bob Pierce, later of World Vision; Bob
Evans, to be founder of Greater European Mission;
Dave Morken and Hube Mitchell, veteran missionaries to Asia; plus several other leaders. After a
gracious meal prepared by Lila and her staff there
were a few testimonies from Navigator men, and
then Dawson took over and unloaded on these
leaders for more than an hour. He hit the basics of
living the Christian life and the importance of the

leader's setting an example for his followers. "How can you expect your followers to be in the Word on a consistent basis and having a daily quiet time if your staff people aren't doing it? And why should your staff men and women be doing it if your key leadership aren't doing it?

"And, gentlemen, do you have any idea why your key personnel aren't memorizing, studying with regularity, and meeting God in a disciplined fashion? It's because you men aren't doing it yourselves. Don't ask others to do that for which you aren't setting the pace."

The hour was late, and Hube Mitchell suggested the possibility of breaking up and meeting again the next morning for a continuing session. Torrey Johnson got to his feet and exploded, "Sit down, Hube. Daws isn't finished with us, and besides, we haven't had the altar call yet!"

In his memoirs, Field-Marshal Montgomery, chief of the British Imperial staff, makes this observation: "I have always held the view that an army is not merely a collection of individuals, with so many tanks, guns, machine-guns, etc., and that the strength of the army is not just the total of all these things added together. The real strength of an army is, and must be, far greater than the sum total of its parts; that extra strength is provided by *morale*, *fighting spirit*, *mutual confidence between the leaders and the led* and especially with the high command, *the quality of comradeship*, and many other intangible spiritual qualities."

This kind of leadership was the desire and prayer of Dawson Trotman for the church of Jesus Christ.

One man gives freely, yet gains
even more; another withholds
unduly, but comes to poverty.
A generous man will prosper;
he who refreshes others will
himself be refreshed.

PROVERBS 11:24-25 (NIV)

Do nothing out of selfish ambi-
tion or vain conceit, but in
humility consider others better
than yourselves. Each of you
should look not only to your
own interests, but also to the
interests of others.

PHILIPPIANS 2:3-4 (NIV)

Chapter 10
A Heart for
the Body

Through his friendship with church leaders, Dawson made a sizable contribution to the body of Christ. Denominational leaders, heads of para-church groups and missionary societies, evangelists, pastors, and teachers could be counted among his close friends. He did not try to make Navigators out of these men and women, but sought instead to serve them in any way he could. His role, he believed, was to encourage them and strengthen their ministry.

Consequently he was very generous in giving, not only of himself but also of Navigator staff members, to other organizations.

Why did Dawson give freely of his precious staff people to help these other works? Part of the answer was that he saw the church as a whole. He detested the competition between Christian organizations and constantly combatted the persistent tendency to build up his own organization and to keep his resources of manpower and finances only for The Navigators. He fought this tendency, in fact, almost to a fault, sometimes depleting his own work.

The organizations that received these men and women, seeing how valuable they were, wanted to keep them, and there were sometimes misunderstandings when Daws wanted them to come back with The Navigators. This "conflict of interest" led Daws to an open policy which said that if and when he "loaned" someone to another organization, it was unconditional. Hence, by the mid 1950s, there were scores of trained and highly qualified Navigators on the staffs of Christian organizations around the world.

This same generous attitude extended to money and materials. Dawson felt that, since most of his concepts and methods were based on the ideas of others, when he shared materials and ideas he was simply giving away what he had received. The very thought of "copyright" was foreign to his nature.

Why clutch to one's self what the entire body of
Christ might benefit from? What he had was the
Lord's, and he desperately wanted everyone to share
in the benefits. Only grudgingly, and out of necessity, did Dawson finally go along with "the mark of
ownership"—because of abuses, and because some
people were profiteering from either the Scripture
memory program or Bible study materials.

    One example of Dawson's generosity in sup-
porting other Christian organizations is that he
would give away money even when it seemed his
own organization most needed it! Prior to moving
Headquarters to Colorado, The Navigators had a
financial drive entitled, "Anchor Home Base." The
Headquarters in Los Angeles needed repair and new
equipment. In the midst of this all-out endeavor, the
annual Forest Home Banquet was staged. Forest
Home, a mountain conference grounds in the San
Bernardino hills of southern California, was the
brain-child of Henrietta Mears of Hollywood Presbyterian Church and Gospel Light Press, a dear
friend of both Daws and Lila Trotman.

    Upon receiving the invitation to this fund-
raising banquet, which was to be held at the Palla-
dium in Hollywood, Daws called and reserved an
entire table for ten. The price wasn't cheap, but
Daws felt the cause was worthy. "Anchor Home
Base" was laid aside for that evening so that The
Navigators could thoroughly enjoy the music, testi-

monies, and a challenge from Miss Mears, who told what God was doing up in the San Bernardino Mountains. After a marvelous meal and a soul-stirring program, it was time for the offering and taking of pledges.

Dawson turned to all of us at the table and asked if we would each write on a piece of paper the amount of commitment that we felt The Navigators ought to make. I sat there pondering the issues: How about our own project, "Anchor Home Base"? Sure we used the Forest Home conference facilities a couple times a year, so what would be right? As I looked around the crowd of over a thousand people, I decided they probably weren't over-committed to other projects as we were, so very freely and with openness of heart, I wrote on my little slip of paper what I thought would be a reasonable share for The Navigators to give.

Daws then collected our pledges, shuffled them with his own, and began to open them one by one. Then he did a most amazing thing. He took his fountain pen and, instead of averaging them, added them all up! He then took the official Forest Home pledge card and filled it out, writing in the *total* of all our pledges as the amount that The Navigators planned to give the following year. Not only was I surprised, but the entire table of staff members was bowled over. On the way out to the car that night, his comment to me was simply, "Freely have we received, freely give!"

"Anchor Home Base" was a huge success, but not without lots of hard work and intense prayer. We had all learned a great lesson that night: you cannot out-give God!

Giving is Christlike

Dawson's commitment to the Scriptures, his constant effort to apply to his life what he learned, and his natural generosity of spirit influenced him to be Christlike in his concern for the whole body. As he saw the splits, competition, and animosities common in local assemblies, missionary organizations, and Christian causes at home and abroad, Daws purposed in his heart that he would lean the other way—he would try to strengthen the hands of his Christian brethren and promote unity.

Among the verses of the Bible that provided a theological underpinning for his emphasis on Christian unity was Philippians 2:5: "Let this mind be in you, which was also in Christ Jesus." The context, verses 1-8, taught Christians to be "likeminded" and have oneness in love. Daws discovered that there were three "let"s in this section of Scripture, and that each "let" was not an option, but a command meaning "make sure." *Make sure* nothing is done through strife or vainglory, *Make sure* each one esteems others better than himself (verse 3), and *Make sure* you have the mind of Christ (verse 5).

In the midst of that setting, verse four shone out

like a vein of gold. "Look not every man on his own things, but every man also on the things of others." Here was the answer to the problem of Christian competition—the balm to heal the splits, bind up the fragments, and reunite the separated!

Once, when one of his young staff was complaining about the shallowness of a certain Christian work, Daws said, very gently, "Tell me, is there anything in that organization that you can praise the Lord for?" The staff member had to admit there were many good things in that Christian work. Daws said, "I have found it a very good policy to praise the Lord for the strengths of a group, and try to help them with their weakness." This was his lifelong attitude.

People were constantly asking Daws to do things which he had to refuse because there wasn't time. But after prayer, he would often relent. Such a request came in 1942 from Cameron Townsend, founder of Wycliffe Bible Translators, who asked Daws to go to Mexico to look over the translators' work and then go to the annual board meeting with any suggestions he wished to offer. The whole process would take two weeks.

"Cam, I'd love to, but I haven't even had time to get down to San Diego and visit our military ministry there. Two weeks is an awfully long time, and besides, there is probably someone else who can do the job better than I."

"But Daws, we need *you*. I want you to do this assignment. Won't you at least pray about it?"

After talking it over with the Lord, Dawson went to Mexico—and also to San Diego! How could he preach concern for others to his staff, he reasoned, if he was not willing to set the pace himself? Had not the Lord commanded him to look not just on his own work of The Navigators, but also on the things of others, like these Bible translators? "Anyhow, what reason can these folks in Mexico have for being generous and giving, if I fail them by setting a selfish and 'me first' example?"

When Dawson and The Navigators began to emphasize giving to others, God blessed them as never before. Daws saw evidence of this blessing in the financial reports, in the multiplication of manpower, and in increasing favor with other Christian works around the world.

To his staff he would often quote Luke 6:38 just as he was ready to leave on another crusade with Billy Graham, or perhaps a board meeting with Wycliffe, or a prolonged tour of the Orient to encourage his visionary buddy, Dick Hillis of Orient Crusades: "Give, and it shall be given unto you; good measure, pressed down, and shaken together, and running over, shall men give into your bosom. For with the same measure that ye mete withal it shall be measured to you again."

Another passage on giving that Dawson loved

to expound was Proverbs 11:24-25: "There is that scattereth, and yet increaseth; and there is that withholdeth more than is meet, but it tendeth to poverty. The liberal soul shall be made fat: and he that watereth shall be watered also himself."

This is the law of the harvest that Dawson felt applied, not just to finances, but also to relationships among churches and other Christian works.

He began a one-man crusade to see if this law could operate in his generation. With everyone too busy, too involved, too hung up on his own little empire, how could the church work together to achieve unity without uniformity? To his own staff in 1954, he stated it quite clearly: "We get the idea that the sun rises and sets on the Navigator work. We don't want that! As in a watch, we are just a small cog in the entire works. Let's make sure we are doing our part and not wondering about the others."

"Look on the things of others. . . ." This command was a deep-seated conviction with Daws. How did this man of God get other works on his heart? Let me suggest three foundational stones in Dawson's life on which was erected, over a period of thirty years, his emphasis on "other works."

An active concern for others

In October of 1947, Dawson wrote about a Navigator conference that featured speakers from other Christian groups. "At the Nav conference, men from various sections of the United States came, making a total of sixty. One of the outstanding features of this week was the prominence given Christian works other than The Navigators. In the light of such passages as Philippians 2:3-4 and 1 Corinthians 12:14 and 21, the Lord has been bringing it increasingly to our attention that He would be honored and glorified through a more complete understanding and cooperation among His various works.

"Although it has been our privilege to have very close cooperation and fellowship with Inter-Varsity, Youth for Christ, and the Young Life Campaign, God favored us at the conference with representative speakers from three other outstanding works, namely, Wycliffe Bible Translators, Moody Institute of Science, and Missionary Aviation Fellowship. These men were invited to give us the latest information concerning the Lord's leading in their section of the vineyard. It is our purpose to familiarize ourselves with those Christian works which honor the Lord and which have the seal and approval of His blessing, not only to learn of their program and to stand by in prayer, but to serve them in other ways as well."

As his thoughts about this conference reveal, Dawson actively sought to involve himself and his staff in the lives of Christians working through other organizations. He often urged the military men he labored with during World War II to join foreign missions groups—and he made it his business to help those men do it, as the following memo clearly shows: "A few of the fellows have written telling us of their desire for a ministry on some foreign field when this conflict is over. Has God laid this desire upon your heart? Are you praying about it? Drop us a line letting us know what is on your heart, and then let us know if there is any way we can help you. In such a case, your name will be added to a definite prayer list so that many of us can be praying for you regarding the future. Would you like to receive literature from some of the foreign mission boards that have a work going in some specific part of the world?"

Dawson was learning that concern for others meant involvement in their lives and ministries. With Jim Rayburn of Young Life back in the 1940s, it meant traveling for weeks:

"We were thrilled as we saw almost 1,000 young people meet together with hearts open with eager anticipation to the messages which God was pleased to supply. Not only in Houston, but hundreds each night in Tyler, San Antonio, Wichita Falls, and Waco . . . all within the balance of that one short week!"

Daws and Jim loved to ride the trains together during those years. There they would exchange stories, laugh together, and pray together as two brothers deeply involved in one common goal—to bring glory to God through the lives of people, young and old. Once Daws was only halfway through his "message" to Jim when it was time to leave Texas for home. Rayburn boarded the train and rode halfway to Los Angeles so he could hear the rest of what Dawson had to share.

Freedom from self-centeredness

Generosity was a quality that Dawson amply demonstrated as well as preached. Selfless giving was always on his mind and heart. When he taught about self-sacrifice, he often stressed the biblical phrase from Philippians 2:3, "Let each esteem other better than themselves." Then he'd explain the passage, "Oh, no! Even if others *are* better than ourselves, how could we treat them that way? Even if we could *find* someone better than ourselves, would it be possible to really *believe* they are better? The human heart just doesn't operate on that wavelength. These verses in Philippians are opposed to natural tendencies. Others *are* better than ourselves. Who in any denomination believes that? We don't believe it! If we do believe it, we don't act like it. I am convinced from the Scriptures and from experience, that knowing the mind of Christ as mentioned in verse five is the climax to the pivotal principle in verse four: Look upon the things of others."

Dawson loved to share Romans 15:5-6 with church leaders and denominational conferences:

"Now the God of patience and consolation grant you to be *likeminded* one toward another according to Christ Jesus: That ye may *with one mind* and one mouth glorify God, even the Father of our Lord Jesus Christ." He would then point out that it has to be more than "*my* church, *my* program, *my* members, or *my* ideas."

Concern for works other than our own is a biblical concept. God is not locked into cultural or economic barriers. As Daws learned more from Scripture about God's concern for others, he decided that God's purpose should be his purpose.

True acceptance of others' differences

The unity and love of believers that Christ prayed for in John 17:21-23, Dawson was convinced, would be one of the greatest advertisements for the gospel:

> That they all may be one; as thou, Father, art in me, and I in thee, that they also may be one in us: that the world may believe that thou hast sent me. And the glory which thou gavest me I have given them; that they may be one, even as we are one: I in them, and thou in me, that they may be made perfect in one; and that the world may know that thou hast sent me, and hast loved them, as thou hast loved me.

Dawson strongly encouraged interdenominational fellowship among evangelicals, despite differences of opinion on secondary matters. He cautioned against becoming so concerned about a narrow view of a certain "truth" (and he was not talking about major doctrines of the faith which define evangelicals) that one forgets to love and pray for a brother who belongs to a different group.

An incident from the Youth for Christ World Congress on Evangelism (in Beatenberg, Switzerland) illustrates the kind of openness and selflessness that Daws placed such great stock in. The initially strained atmosphere at the Congress was due in large part to the self-imposed segregation of the various national groups. Representatives from around the world had gathered to be "one in Christ," but it wasn't working out that way. Western Europeans were clustering together off to one side; Americans were stepping into the spotlight with fancy clothes and a moneyed appearance; the reserved English were quietly drinking their tea. One evening, veteran missionary Hubert Mitchell asked for the podium and then called up a very humble servant of God from south India. Hube blamed the tense atmosphere on self-centeredness on the part of both East and West. Then quoting Matthew 25:36, he took off his jacket and asked the Indian, who had come with only a light sweater, to try it on. The fit was perfect! Hube gave his brother the jacket, and amid considerable prayer and emotion, the walls of separation broke down. Christ-centeredness took over. The message was clear to all: We must think in terms of the whole body of Christ, not just our narrow area of specialization.

In a hard-hitting section of a message entitled "Our Resources in Christ," Daws zeroed in on petty divisiveness: "A preacher gets up in the morning and he goes to his little study and he opens his Bible and reads a few verses, and he has a little word of prayer. And he says, 'Lord, bless me today and make me a blessing and bless the people of my church.'

"Across the street is another little church. It's a different denomination. There are a few external things, a few things that the pastor does in this one that that one doesn't do, and vice versa. But somehow the fact that the other man doesn't quite see it like this man does has drawn a barrier. That man has prayed . . . this man prays. Who is he praying to? He is praying to the same Person, and he's asking the same thing.

"Across the street and down a little is another church. It's the second something or the third something or the Grace Street something, and the preacher prays. He gets up from prayer and walks out. As he goes out the door on his way to the car he glances up and he sees a sign on the church across the street: 'Revival Services Begin July 30th.' He goes down the street mumbling, 'Revival! Doesn't that geezer know that you don't *create* revival services? Why doesn't he put "Evangelistic Services"? What a stupe! To think he can create revival!' You know who that man is he's talking about? That's his fellow soldier. That's his brother. That's the servant of the Lord and Savior he spoke to that morning.

"July 30th comes, and they have a good speaker. Strange how people flock to speakers, isn't it? But he's a good speaker, they've got a good program, so the Christians are coming. One out of twenty brings somebody. It's announced in the morning paper that there was an overflow in the little church. Is this fellow over there happy? No! 'Doesn't use the right methods; got the wrong message.'"

Dawson deplored this negative attitude. *What* we believe often divides us, he felt, but *who* we believe unites us.

The church—Christ's body—is *one* body composed of many members with diverse functions and gifts. Daws saw this scriptural teaching clearly. He loved the twelfth chapter of 1 Corinthians. He studied it, memorized it, meditated on it, and then went out to preach and practice it. "No schism" was his clarion call. Verse twenty-five was the heart of his text: "that the members should have the same care one for another." There should be mutual concern, mutual interest, sympathetic relationships with one another. Verse twenty-six became a living part of his personal life, his family life, and that of the organization which he headed: "And if one member suffers, all the parts share the suffering; if one member is honored, all the members share in the enjoyment of it" (*The Amplified Bible*).

Toward the end of his life, Dawson asked Bill Bright to speak to the Navigator staff: "Bill, give a hard-hitting message on evangelism. I thank God for sending you and Campus Crusade so close to us in The Navs. We have an eternal preoccupation with follow-up, and because of it we get so busy, because so many ask us for help, that we get *weak in evangelism*. That is your strength, evangelism, and your gang probably don't do much with follow-up. The two of us balance each other off well. I think that's why God wants us to work with other parts of the church. Instead of looking off and criticizing their weak points, let's work together and glean from each other the strong points. We all need each other!"

Dawson's ability to overlook petty and potentially divisive differences grew out of his genuine concern for others. Bill Bright said of Dawson, "Daws knew that the more he helped others—selflessly, with pure motivation—the more God would bless and anoint him, and return to him many times that which he seemingly gave away to others. He was very generous to me when we first started at UCLA on the campus of that great university. Overnight we saw scores of students coming into the kingdom. I was a relatively new Christian, and Dawson had agreed to serve as a member of our board of directors, along with Henrietta Mears,

Dick Halverson, and several others. Before long there were so many people coming to Christ that I was spending day and night trying to follow them up, and one day I sent out an SOS to Daws asking if he would help. For a period of many weeks he came early every Saturday morning about 6:00 to meet with the scores of young people coming to know Christ, and he assisted me in helping to disciple them. He also loaned to us some of his key young men and women to help. The entire ministry of Campus Crusade has benefited because he so freely gave of himself in those early years. His example played a major role in helping me to see the big picture of what God wants."

... Ye shall be witnesses unto
me both in Jerusalem, and in all
Judaea, and in Samaria, and
unto the uttermost part of the
earth.

ACTS 1:8

I love him deeply for the things
that he shared about the needs
of the world, for the fact that
the Lord used Daws to put the
world upon my heart.

DOUG COE

Chapter 11
A Passion for the World

Up in the beautiful Sierra Nevada mountains of central California, at Hume Lake Bible Conference in 1949, Dawson was asking a question that searched the depths of his listeners' souls: "What's on your heart?" Listen to what he said to those eager young people that bright summer morning: "Why should you have a world vision? Because it is the heart of God! It may not be the heart of our *churches*, nor our *schools*, nor our Christian *families*, but the fact remains, it is the *heart of God*! Let's look together to-day into the Holy Scriptures and see what is the mind of Christ. If we don't base it all on the Bible, we sure don't have a solid foundation.

"There's no use trying to get a world vision until you know how to. Let's look at Acts 1:8—that's the 'how to.' I love the way the Holy Spirit packs into one sentence the whole story. '*Ye shall receive power*.' That's what the disciples of Christ wanted. 'The Holy Spirit shall come upon you.' That's what they needed. 'Be my witnesses.' That was to be their job. 'Unto me.' That was the objective.

"Where was all this to happen? 'Beginning in Jerusalem, in Judaea, and Samaria, and the utter-most part of the world.' There it is. There's the plan, gang!

"If the gospel will work here at home, it will work out there. It won't work out there until we do it here. The very plan we are given for missionary work often starts wrong. I was taught to deal with strangers, hitchhikers and cold contacts, but I wasn't told how to witness to my family, my neighbors, nor the fellows I worked with at the lumber company.

"I believe the Navigator work is strong today because our men started with the fellows they knew. Those they lived with and worked with in the Navy. That's where we started. Oh, how I rejoiced! Not with all the meetings, nor the numbers coming to our home for Bible study, nor the attendance in the ship library, but that the Navs were sharing and witnessing first of all in their own Jerusalems. Is it any wonder that after the war was over in the mid forties these very men got their formal training and spread throughout the world? The vision of a world starts with a vision of *one* individual. If you can care for one, God can give you a burden for the world."

Years later, Dawson was still going strong on world vision. Doug Coe, of Washington, D.C., remembered this drive of Dawson's: "I suppose along with hundreds of other young men, I was most impressed with Dawson's vision for the world. I can remember standing alongside him as we held up a large map and he would have us put our fingers on different countries. Then we would pray for that country, that laborers would be raised up in China, Korea, Kenya, South Africa, Europe, and Latin America.

"And so on around the world we would pray . . . large countries and those that it was difficult to see the names of. I thought it was kind of a stupid exercise in the beginning, but I have to tell you, I find myself doing it today in exactly the same way.

"Often as I travel from nation to nation these days, those thoughts about Dawson recur—the large world map; those times of prolonged prayer for needs, laborers, missionary organizations; and his heavy burden for the lost. I love him deeply for the things that he shared about the needs of the world, for the fact that the Lord used Daws to put the world upon my heart."

This vision of the world was in Daws's thinking even back during the years of World War II. One of Dawson's team told about the time in 1943 when Cameron Townsend of Wycliffe was speaking in the Church of the Open Door in Los Angeles. "We had brought up a gang of sailors from Long Beach to hear Mr. Townsend and his missionary concern for the tribes of the world which still didn't have a written language, and hence they had no Bible. It seemed to me that there were about one thousand languages yet to be reduced to writing. Right in the midst of his message, Cam looked over to where we were sitting and said, 'Daws, I want five hundred of your sailors to get their training when they are out of the service and I want you to have them ready to come and join us in this venture.' Cam paused for a moment as though he was going to ask for a commitment that night, and then Daws spoke up, 'Cam, if it be God's will, we'll provide you those five hundred men.'

"Cam shot back, 'It *is* God's will—you go ahead and start making plans to get them!'"

A well-known Southern Baptist pastor related this beautiful memory: "'Daws, what do you have on your heart?' I asked him the very morning that he died. His answer was simple and yet profound: 'The world.' I have never heard anyone else say that in answer to a question like that. I know he was right, and I know that was exactly what he had on his heart the day he went to be with the Lord."

"That all may hear"
Few people have world vision. We tend to concentrate on our own field and shut out the rest of the world. One veteran missionary to the Orient told how Daws impressed the worldwide scope of the Great Commission on him: "On the eve of my going to China, Dawson called me to his home in South Pasadena, California. I knelt down and prayed and Dawson put his hands upon me and prayed. It was my commissioning by God and by Dawson to go to China as God's ambassador. As Daws prayed, I'll never forget some of the words: 'Lord, I pray that you will put upon this young man the same thing that is on Your heart—*the world*.' Most people he knew had one country upon their heart—but not the world.

"I went to China with that vision. I was there just six months and the Communists came and took over China, and we all had to leave. All the missionaries had to go home. This was a very traumatic thing, because in order to become a member of some missionary societies, you had to believe that God had called you to the physical country called China. Now China was closing to the gospel of Jesus Christ. Hundreds of missionaries who had been called by God were now pulling out in turmoil. Praise the

Lord, Daws had ingrained into my heart 'bifocal vision'—the ability to see clearly right where you are but also to look up and see the big harvest fields that are also white unto reaping."

A favorite expression of Dawson's was, "Reach beyond." This was his way of saying, "After you have finished the little job where you are, be ready for the next and then the next. Be content where you are, but always be ready for the next move by the Holy Spirit." Because so many hours in his youth were spent in the local pool halls, he often used an illustration from billiards: "Think your second and third shot. Plan for the next play."

Dawson was convinced that this world could be reached for Christ in his generation. "That all may hear" was his battle call. He had plans that were big and exciting, and sometimes intimidating, to his staff and fellow workers. He felt that every church, every Christian organization, every member of the Body, had a responsibility to carry out the Great Commission of Jesus Christ.

He was convinced that the job of reaching the world would be carried out most effectively by "multiplication of disciples." This strategy would enlist the laymen; it would get everyone working in the harvest fields while training still more faithful members to become laborers.

"Low profile" describes Daws at this point. He was well known in the North American continent, but relatively unknown by the church in other parts of the world. He never tried to promote himself, his materials, or his organization. There was no public relations department for The Navigators. Quietly and in an orderly way they went about their business: "To know Christ and to make Him known."

Although he never promoted himself, Daws could get very excited about promoting the Great Commission. To be instrumental in getting people around the world to be their very best for Christ—this really turned Dawson on! The horizon of his vision was unlimited. Those close to him were caught up in his plans and the convictions that the goals he set could be achieved.

Our ultimate goal

"What is our ultimate goal?" Daws consistently asked this question of individual Christians, churches, and organizational leaders. Prior to his conversion, Daws's goal was to make as much money as possible so that he could have a good time —a goal at which he was fairly successful. When Christ came into his life, a whole new value system took over. His goal then became to win as many people to Christ as possible. In his attempt to make up for lost time, he plunged into "soulwinning," which for him at that time meant getting names written down, cards signed, and prayers made.

It soon became evident to Dawson, however,

that this business-like approach to evangelism just wasn't very effective. "I got the shock of my life," he later reflected. "I saw some of these men after a few months or years. They certainly weren't God's converts—they were mine. I had gotten them to go through the motions and say the right words, but their hearts weren't changed by the grace of God."

As a result, Daws began an intensive program of personal growth. His goal was Scripture memorization and Bible study. The words of D.L. Moody became his new goal: "Be the man whom God can use." Along about the same time came such goals as, "Be a member of a church that has the touch of God upon it and whose members are loving, caring, and giving." "To know Christ and to make Him known."

Then a change began to creep into his teaching. Dawson's talks in the late forties increasingly revealed that his goal had become, "every man and woman a reproducer for Christ."

But he began to realize that even this goal was not the ultimate one, although it was moving in the right direction.

What is the ultimate goal for the Christian? Dawson became convinced that he knew what that goal was. Beginning with Genesis 12:3, "in thee shall all families of the earth be blessed," he traced the plan of God through the ages, beginning with the story of Abraham, the history of the children of Israel, the prophets, the life of Christ, and ending up in Acts

1:8: "witnesses unto me both in Jerusalem, and in all Judaea, and in Samaria, and unto the uttermost part of the earth."

The ultimate goal, as Daws saw it, was to reach "every creature," thus bringing glory to God. The *only* barrier he saw to this goal was unbelief. In May of 1948, he reflected, "The job is tremendous! We've done the one percent. The ninety-nine percent is still left. Had it not been that my heart has been stayed on Him, I'd consider the needs of the world and the cry of people everywhere so great that I'd be frightened. But God loves the world, and starting with twelve apparently poorly prepared disciples, he told them that the world was their parish. Now, it is 1900 years later, and I know the job can be done; by His grace it shall be done. Our big project in the years just ahead is to pool our resources and personnel in America and begin to get folks prepared for the field—thinking follow-up and follow-through in connection with all these dear people."

Accomplishing the mission

Just six years before, at the beginning of World War II, Dawson had been writing to his men scattered throughout the U.S. military establishments: "Navigators, with the training that God is giving you on the firing line for our beloved country, for the ever-increasing burden that is yours to reach the unreached . . . I challenge you to meet His challenge,

'Whom shall I send?' with your answers, 'Lord, here am I . . . send me!'"

Dawson believed that each generation was commanded to carry out the Great Commission. He believed that the disciples carried it out in their generation in the first century: "Not long after the giving of the Commission, while most all of those men who had been with Jesus on the mountain just outside of Jerusalem were still alive, the apostle Paul is writing to a tiny church fellowship in another continent and he's saying,

"'We give thanks to God always for you. . . . For from you sounded out the word of the Lord not only in Macedonia and Achaia, but *also in every place* your faith to Godward is spread abroad; so that we need not to speak any thing'—1 Thessalonians 1:2 and 8. Notice that the apostles started with about 120 people. How many people do we have today? There are tens of thousands of believers in America alone. Almost every one has a concordance and all kinds of Christian books about the Bible. We've got radios, churches, education, and transportation. Are we doing today what the Thessalonian church did two thousand years ago? *No!* I go on record this morning, June 26, 1949, to say that I believe *we can do it in this generation!*"

The key obstacle to carrying out this commission, Daws pointed out, was failure to believe in God's promises—which could be traced to a weak or lacking devotional life. "Crossing the ocean doesn't make a missionary. If you haven't won the battle of the quiet time here at home, you won't have any more time or discipline to get it built in overseas. If you haven't won victory over temptation . . . won a soul to Christ . . . or trained yourself to study the Scriptures here in good old U.S.A., there's no reason to believe it's going to happen, like a miracle, four thousand miles away!"

But, Dawson admitted, it took him many years to gain a world vision. "I never used to preach world vision in my earlier years. Why? Because I didn't have it. I didn't have the faith to have it. I wanted it, but didn't know how or where to get it. My biggest problem was in not seeing what God was capable of doing. That is when I asked Walt to join me in praying each morning for two hours before work and on Sundays . . . three hours early in the day. One hundred hours—you can ask God for a lot in that number of hours.

"We sure didn't start out praying big, but we ended up praying, 'Lord, allow us to serve you in *every continent* of the world.' We didn't know all that we were asking for, but God did, and that's all that counts. Things began to change when one of us, and I don't remember who really said it, remarked to the other, 'Let's get a map of the world.'

"That changed my whole perspective. From then on, and it's more true today than ever before, my prayer has been, 'Bring us, O God, a band of strong, rugged soldiers of the Cross, with an eye single for Your glory.'"

Daws would then tell how the Navigator work began in one little city of the world. That tiny town was a self-contained unit with its own power plant, water system, food supply, and communications system. There were about one hundred men in that town who knew the Lord and had a strong desire to make Him known. Then one day, quite by surprise, on December 7th, 1941, that city was bombed by the Japanese. Many boys were killed or seriously wounded. The town was "totalled." It sank out of sight, but what was left of those one hundred Christian men were scattered throughout the United States Navy, preaching the Word of God and reaching others for the Savior.

That little city was a battleship, the U.S.S. *West Virginia*. And the dispersing of those men was divine strategy during the war years. Years later, when the peace treaties were signed, there were hundreds of men ready to answer Daws's prayer that he had prayed in the hills of southern California years before.

Daws's method of instilling world vision in an audience was to lay a foundation from the Bible, for he knew that a challenge with any lesser authority would soon evaporate and become a forgotten emotion.

"*Who* should we try to reach, and *How much* of the world is to be our parish?" His outline would look like this:

Who are we to reach?

The Heathen nations	Psalm 96:3
The Gentiles	Isaiah 60:3,11
All Nations	Romans 16:26

How far are we to go?

Ends of the earth	Acts 13:47
Uttermost parts	Acts 1:8
All the world	Mark 16:15
Till earth filled with His knowledge	Isaiah 11:9

Once he had put up this outline, Daws would explain to his audience what he felt was the practical key to accomplishing this immense task. "How are we, in the twentieth century, going to do this? Shall we flood the nations of the world with foreign missionaries? We here in America have already sent out over ten thousand missionaries in the last 150 years. Add to that the thousands sent by other countries like England, Scotland, the Scandinavian countries, and various other European nations. . . . What's it going to take to get the job done?

"Do you know, gang, what one of the major problems is? We are *foreigners* to other countries of the world. We don't know their language, their culture, their religions. We don't eat like they eat; we don't dress like they dress. All of those things are barriers, or at best, little stumbling stones.

"To know what a hummingbird is thinking, I would have to be a hummingbird. To know why a donkey acts, reacts, and does the things a donkey does, I would have to be born a donkey. It is no different in China, Africa, Latin America, or India. The Chinese can reach the Chinese far better than the Caucasian. Would it surprise you to hear that there is nothing in the Bible that says members of the white race are to be the only missionaries?

"The Great Commission was given to *all* people. Koreans are to have a world vision; not just for the Orient or wherever there are pockets of their Korean people; the whole world is theirs. Anything less is not good enough. No matter where I live, where I was born and raised, I am to be a recruiting officer for the needs of all the world. Those are my standing orders.

"It starts with a vision for one person. Young people, you will not have a world vision till you have a vision for one person. You've heard me tell it before, but it bears repeating: You'll never have a world vision till you have a vision for one country. You'll never have a vision for one country till you have a vision for one city. You'll never have a vision for one city till you see clearly one city block. That one city block never comes into focus till you see one house. You'll never have a vision for one family in that house, till you have a vision for one person!"

This naturally brought Dawson back to personal evangelism and the concept of one-on-one follow-up and multiplication. Dawson challenged people to pray about the mission field in their own home, their neighborhood, community, work situation, and church. He personally started evangelizing those in his "backyard"—the men of the United States Navy. But even before that, there were those little boys in his Sunday school class, and the teenagers in Christian Endeavor. "Start where you are," he'd say, "and God will enlarge your ministry." He also liked to quote, "You are responsible for the *depth of your life*; let God be responsible for the *breadth of your ministry*."

Daws believed in the power of prayer to give one a vision for the world. "Pray ye therefore the Lord of the harvest, that he will send forth labourers into his harvest" (Matthew 9:38). The very ones whom Christ asked to pray (in chapter 9) were the ones he thrust forth (in chapter 10). Daws, therefore, constantly emphasized the importance of prayer in developing a passion for reaching the world: "It's great to have a packet of memory verses that you are working into your life; it's thrilling to meet a man or woman who has conquered difficult and disciplined Bible study methods, but you show me your *prayer list* and that will indicate right fast how deep and broad is your spiritual life. A person's prayer page is the indicator of his world vision. That's where your heart is. *What you are praying for is what you are living for."*

When Dawson boarded a plane in Hong Kong on April 19, 1948 to head back to the U.S., he left many new and old friends in China. Andrew Gih, who served as his interpreter for most of his meetings and whom he came to love dearly, took over the last meetings in Chengtu when Daws was confined to the hospital with a lacquer poisoning (much like a severe case of poison oak). Of those days in the Chinese hospital, Daws wrote, "I'm down, but not out; believe you me, I'm not complaining. I've seen enough suffering by those people who can never hope for relief to forever quiet my complaining.

"What a privilege to be in the home of Dick Hillis and his lovely family. On my last day with them, I heard a little prayer which will forever ring in my ears. We were finishing breakfast, and their little six-year-old girl was asked to say a word of prayer. In typical fashion, she prayed for everyone she could think of, including Mr. Trotman. And then she finished off with something like this: '. . . and dear God, we know that there are going to be lots of people in heaven, but God, we want lots more!'"

"We want more!" That was the consuming passion of Dawson's life and ministry.

With his bifocal vision for the individual close at hand as well as the masses of the world, Daws wrote the following: "There are millions of thirsty souls. There is sufficient water in the 'well of salvation' to adequately quench every one of those thirsty souls. God is looking for vessels through which He might transmit this living water to them. It matters not regarding the apparent outward value of the vessel or the seeming lack of worth. The only kind of vessel that He can use to carry this living water to these dying souls is a vessel that is 'meet for the Master's use,' that is one that is first cleansed of sin and then emptied of self.

"Perhaps this truth can be more readily made clear by a simple illustration. Let us imagine a clear, cool, crystal stream of living water flowing beside a broad way. There comes a tired, worn-out, thirsty traveler. He sees the water, but it flows under such circumstances as to make it impossible for him to reach this stream with his mouth. He spies three vessels: a golden goblet, a silver pitcher, and a tin cup.

"Upon investigation he finds that the golden goblet is filled with something else. The silver pitcher is empty, apparently ready for service but is soiled within; the tin cup alone is clean and emptied. We leave it to you to decide which one he chooses. To rightly get at the heart of this great truth, meditate on: Acts 24:16; 2 Timothy 2:20-21; and 1 Corinthians 1:26-30. Which kind are you?"

Lord, if anything has been said
which is from You which You
want to impart to these hearts,
do cause it to remain and
become a part of their lives.

DAWSON TROTMAN

Chapter 12
A Final Message

On June 18, 1956, Dawson Trotman triumphantly entered into the presence of the Lord while saving the life of a young lady from drowning in the icy waters of Schroon Lake, New York.

The following condensed message was given by Daws to a Navigator conference at Glen Eyrie, Colorado on June 14, 1956—just four days before his death. This talk reflects the concerns that were uppermost in his mind and heart and, in a sense, summarizes the Navigator ministry. Today, nearly thirty years later, this message still outlines the basic thrust of The Navigators.

"The Big Dipper"

"I would like to share with you a little incident that happened on one of my trips around the world in May, 1948.

"I was in Paris, France, and had an engagement with Stacey Woods, the leader of Inter-Varsity Christian Fellowship. The night I met him on the streets of Paris it was almost midnight, and by 3:00 a.m. we had been accosted thirteen times by young women of the street. Right there I discovered that it wasn't spiritually healthy to be out on the streets of Paris alone at night.

"I had an extra day to stay, so I just gave the following night to the Lord. I decided to go up on the roof of the George V Hotel, so I pulled one of the blankets off my bed along with a pillow, dusted off a place up there, and swished out the blanket. It was a beautiful starry night, and I lay out on the flat of my back looking up into the heavens and talked with the Lord. The night wasn't too cool nor was it too warm just to be there and reflect on the heavens and who had created all these things and called them all by name.

"While I was looking at the stars and thinking, I was praying and meditating on some Scripture and letting Him speak to me through the Word, and I prayed something like this: 'Lord, is there something in the Navigator work that we are omitting or failing to do that is displeasing to You? Is there something you don't want us to be doing? What are we doing that brings you pleasure?'

"...I happened to be looking up there at the Big Dipper. I studied those seven stars with four forming the bucket and the three out there as the handle. As I was thinking and meditating, an idea came to me (I have always used associations to help in remembering things. People can remember the Christ-centered, Spirit-filled life, for example, if they can see a picture of a wheel.) The very heart of the Christian life is the Wheel, and so as I was looking at the Big Dipper, I put that principle on the pivotal star of the dipper. It carries the weight between the handle and the bucket. It is the lever that supplies the hinge or support for all the rest.

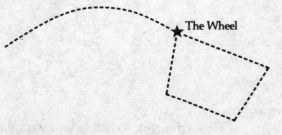

The Wheel

"Then my eyes dropped down to the star just below. And then I thought, 'We already know of the main basic things of the Scriptures, prayer, obedience and witnessing.' We in The Navigators stress the Bible quite a bit. The five ways of getting a grip on Scripture are pictured in the Hand—knowing it by hearing, reading, studying, memorizing, and meditating. Each one of these is independent, and yet all five are dependent upon the others. If any one is missing, you have a deformed hand. We must have all five methods of intake if as soldiers of the Cross, we are to handle aright the sword of the Spirit.

"These first two stars are the backbone of our work—the balanced Christian life revolving around the Lord Jesus Christ, and the importance of the *Word of God*. Without these, there is no production for God.

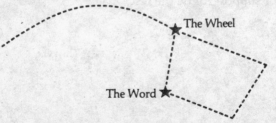

"... Then I thought, 'What's another emphasis of The Navigators?' Why, naturally ... evangelism.

It's the very heartbeat of our ministry. As in the dipper that I saw in the sky, the third star is the scoop. It's the blade with which you dig. Without evangelism you haven't got anything. It is the cutting edge. Our aim was for new Christians to learn to reach out to others; otherwise it is like being born sterile, if they don't reproduce. Even before we began to work with Billy Graham in his big campaigns around the world, we were really hitting it hard on evangelism . . . whether personal, or group, or mass, or any type of evangelism that is suggested in the Bible or that the Lord will be pleased to prosper. Whatever it is, we're for it!

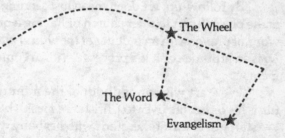

"... You reach out with a shovel and scoop up, but what do you need on that shovel to make a real dipper? We want a backside to hold in the contents. You need something to conserve that which you have picked up. This is the fourth star that I saw that night in Paris.

The thing that holds your people once you've won them to Christ is follow-up. I know many of you are familiar with the fact that the Navs are strong in their emphasis on conserving the fruits of evangelism.

"By follow-up, we don't mean just sending in a name of a convert to their church or having a quick word of prayer with an inquirer at the altar. Follow-up is an attitude . . . it is a process . . . it is a commitment.

"We start with an individual the minute he turns his or her life over to Christ. . . . He is a baby. We start just like a mother starts with her baby when it is born. The doctor doesn't say, 'Well, now that's a healthy baby boy. I can see you won't have to bother with that one for about a week. Let's see, this is Sunday. You sit there, mother, and next Sunday be sure to come back and we'll see how your baby is doing.' Why is it that we leave a new baby Christian alone a whole week until he gets to the next service or

meeting—if he does? Who can tell me who's busy
with him right away? The old devil! And he isn't
going to say, 'Let's have fair play here. This poor
baby isn't getting taken care of properly. I'll not
tackle him until a week from Monday.' That just
doesn't happen.

"We believe in follow-up. These last two stars
form the dipper and they are what we call reproduction . . . evangelism and follow-up. But there will be
no reproduction until there is production. The
building must be built on the foundation. These four
stars make up the main emphasis of life and ministry.

"Well, now, you've got a dipper. I'm still lying
there on my back on the hotel roof . . . just looking up
and studying while my mind is running along the
three stars of the handle of the Big Dipper. Let's see:
The Christ-centered, Spirit-filled life. Yep, we're
strong in that. We're always trying to get folks into a
strong devotional life, always trying to get people
into the Word of God, always fighting to get them to
get the message out, and always fighting to get them
to take care of the ones they win. Well, now, what
else do we really believe is basic? What else is there
that we are willing to give our lives for?

". . . One thought crowded into my mind—
pacesetting. It is the one thing that gives a handle to
production and reproduction. I realize that pacesetting is a poor word. Let's get another word or two.
How about 'example,' or 'your life the embodiment

of the first four stars'? Other words you might use are, 'pattern,' 'model,' or 'prototype.' To give you Scriptures on it, let me start with Matthew 4:19. Jesus didn't say to his men, 'Now listen to me and I'll make you fishers of men.' What did He say? Not 'listen to me,' but 'follow me.' In other words, we learn by seeing, not just by hearing. That's one of the problems of much of our present-day education. We sit at desks for twelve years and primarily listen. Teaching is definitely not just telling, but it's also showing. Here is a super-duper verse in the Bible on the subject—Philippians 4:9. . . .

"Now listen to this . . . this is dynamite: 'Those things that you have learned and heard and received and *seen in me* do, and the God of peace will be with you.' That's the Christian life, gang. Would you rather have for a teacher a person who only knew a little of the Bible but it was part of his life, and he lived it, or a man who knew the Bible from Genesis to Revelation who wasn't living it? How many will take the man who knew less but who's living it? And the whole Word is that way. But it doesn't have to be either-or. . . . I'll go for both-and. I want to be a man who both knows the Bible from cover to cover and also lives it!

"Paul, the great teacher, the great evangelist, the great apostle, said, 'Whatever you have seen in me, do it.' Someone has said, 'I'd rather see a sermon than hear one any day; I'd rather you would walk with me than merely point the way; The eye's a better pupil and more willing than the ear; Fine counsel's oft confusing, but example's always clear.'

"I love that, and yet, it's so easy to go off to school and tank up on a bunch of facts and figures and then try to go transmit those facts and figures by the voice or by the written page. Jesus didn't do it. He was always leading by example. 'As Christ suffered, leaving us an *example* that you should follow in His steps'—1 Peter 2:21. I find it much easier to talk with sinners because Jesus did. It makes the difference. And that's what we mean by pacesetting.

"Let me share another verse on pacesetting. First Thessalonians 1:5 says this: 'Our gospel came not unto you in word only, but it came to you in power and in the Holy Spirit and in much assurance.' It came with assurance because you, the Thessalonians, 'know what manner of men we were among you.' It isn't that everything you hear me say you may see me do, but there will be just enough that you do see . . . that you can tell whether we are sterling silver or just silver-plated.

"Just one other verse, 1 Corinthians 11:1: 'Be ye followers of me even as I am of the Lord.' Paul knew that he followed the Lord, and he knew that if the people in Corinth would step where he was stepping that they would step where Jesus stepped. To follow Paul was to be in step with Jesus Christ. I can't give that verse very often, but it's a goal. . . . It's the desire of good dads and mothers. It's the very heart of good teaching. How would you like it if all the Christians who found the Savior and grew had the same strong points and the same weak points as you? If you knew they were going to have them couldn't you just work hard on those weak ones? A father hears his little boy tell a buddy, 'When I grow up, I want to be just like my daddy!' Whether it be in living the Christ-centered life, or a consistent commitment to the Scriptures; whether it be daily sharpening the cutting edge of evangelism or discipline to nurture my converts until they are mature in Christ . . . all these factors demand pacesetting and example-setting on our part.

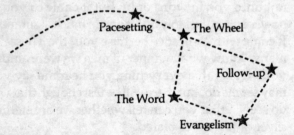

". . . 'Lord, what is something else big that's on Your heart?' I asked, and a verse of Scripture went through my mind. 'Let this mind be in you which was also in Christ. . . .'

"I didn't have my Bible with me up there on the roof top, but I had many portions of it hidden in my heart. Boy, does that help! When the Bible is in your heart, it's with you twenty-four hours a day, whether in a Communist prison camp, walking down a dark lane, or on top of a hotel in Paris. 'Let this mind be in you which was also in Christ. . . .' The context popped into my mind. Yes, that is an emphasis with us. . . . We want to be servants to others. But the verses just before verse 5 in Philippians 2 stood out bright and clear . . . even as the middle star on the handle of the Big Dipper. Put these verses down in big letters. This is the missing link in the body of Jesus Christ. The Lord so burdened me with that concept found in verses 3 and 4 that I could hardly keep back the tears. I'm thankful that it had already begun in our ministry, but it wasn't strong enough. It was out on the fringe, not at the center. 'Let nothing be done through strife or vainglory, but in lowliness of mind *let each esteem other better than themselves.*'

"Who do you know who truly believes that others (churches, organizations, fellowships, denominations, mission boards, ministries) are better than they are? A sure cure for criticism: 'Let each esteem others better than themselves.' Now the very next verse in Philippians 2 says, 'Look not every man on his own things, but every man on the things of others.' This means what others are doing—their words, their plans, and their ministry. The tendency today is for me to feel that my denomination is superior, and all others are inferior. The reason that

idea affects you negatively is because you *know* the
Methodists are better than all these others, because
you are a Methodist. That would be true whether
you are a Baptist, Lutheran, or Catholic. You never
hear anybody saying the other denominations are
better. It's the same thing that every nationality feels.
Superiority! We all feel better than others. It's human
nature, it's part of our heredity. Yet in God's sight,
they are all the same. The yellow man isn't any better
than a black man or a white, nor is a white man better
than any other man. But just try to make yourself
believe that, or even worse, try to get others to really
believe it.

"There emerged in my heart and mind that night
the thought that The Navigators must not work just
for The Navigators, nor try to build the Navigator
organization, but must work for the church—not
just *a* church, but *the* church . . . all churches. Maybe
they don't agree on certain points of theology or
order of worship, or doctrine, but any church where
Jesus Christ is Lord . . . let's get behind them and push
them. The minute we hear of another Christian
work or ministry, we should take time to find out,
not what's wrong with it, but what's right about it
and encourage them and give them a lift. We've emphasized it, but not nearly enough. I jotted down on
the back of a piece of paper what it's costing me to
have this emphasis, and it looks something like this:
"Board of Directors, Wycliffe Bible Translators

Summer School of Linguistics
Missionary Aviation Fellowship
Missionary Communication Service
International Students, Inc.
Youth for Christ, International
The Billy Graham Team

"Each of these means anywhere from one to three trips across the country a year. None of this is Navigator business, but it is the King's business, and that's what we are involved in. It's costing us, but Proverbs 11:24-25 is still true: 'There is that scattereth, and yet increaseth; and there is that withholdeth more than is meet, but it tendeth to poverty. The liberal soul shall be made fat: and he that watereth shall be watered also himself.'

"A person just can't out-give God. In 1950 I was to take a world trip costing $3100 and we didn't have a dollar for it when I ordered the ticket. The weekend came when I was to have the money or they would cancel the ticket. I prayed and waited upon the Lord. We were in Washington, D.C. with the Billy Graham Campaign, helping with the counseling and follow-up. Saturday afternoon Billy called me into his hotel room: 'Dawson, you're going around the world pretty soon, aren't you?'

"'Well, I'm supposed to leave on Tuesday.'

"'Got your ticket, yet?'

"'Not really—I need a little cash.'

"Billy thought for a moment and then said, 'You

know what we'll do? Tonight after the regular offering, I'll call you up to the platform and have you give
a short testimony and I'll tell the folks what you are
going to be doing in the coming weeks around the
world. We have been here in D.C. for three weeks
and haven't done this yet. . . . We'll take a retiring offering for you and your work.'

"Boy, was that something! Well, Billy had me
up there, he said some nice words, and then he told
the audience he wanted them to help send me
overseas. 'Mr. Trotman will be here at the front of
the auditorium. . . . You come up, shake his hand
and leave something in his hand for the trip.'

"The first fifty to the front after the service were
cute little 'bobby soxers' who wanted my autograph
in their Crusade Songbook. They had me in a corner
for forty minutes! No chance for anyone to put
anything in my hand!

"Pretty soon a big old burly guy comes up and
rescues me and says, 'Come over here and take a
look.' There in a suitcase was an overflowing pile of
money. People were still coming up, and the meeting
had been over for almost an hour. They gave me a
police escort to the hotel, loaded suitcase and all.
Twenty-seven hundred dollars in pennies, nickels,
dimes, quarters, and bills. There was $1200 in one-
dollar bills, plus some fives and tens!

"As I sat there on the edge of the bed counting
the money, I thought, 'Isn't that strange that the Lord

would send $2700 and not the needed $3100? He could have done it just as easily as He fed the five thousand people with the five loaves and two fishes.'

"But God knew that I couldn't buy my ticket until Monday morning, and Sunday I was in the Crusade meeting and different men and women came and said, 'Mr. Trotman, there were so many people up front last night, and since I wanted to meet you personally, I waited until today to slip this into your hand.' Late that afternoon, after getting back to the hotel room, I counted what was in my right coat pocket. I'll give you seventy-five guesses how much there was in my hand. You're right—$400. The total was $3100!

"We put our time and energy in these other works of God and He looks down from heaven and says, 'Dawson, you can't out-give Me.'

"Gang, don't ever get into the Nav work if you are going to let the sun rise and the sun set on the Nav work. If it's in your heart and mind to serve the Lord's people by whatever stripe they may be called . . . if they belong to Him and love Him . . . be open to the possibility of helping them as much as possible. We know this is what is on His heart and what He wants. Frankly, if there is anything that He doesn't want or if I can find out that He doesn't want it, I want to de-emphasize it or kick it out. My heart is open.

"Do you think the Lord is going to let you down when you try to fulfill some of these calls and demands from other parts of His body? He can't! Not if we're obeying His Word.

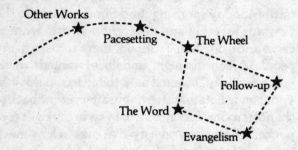

". . . Let me share with you about that last star, away out there on the end of the Big Dipper handle. It had now been two or three hours that I had been on that hotel roof, but I wasn't even aware of the cooling night air. I said to myself, 'World vision has got to go out there on that last star. That's as far as you can get.' This is the seventh emphasis that God laid upon my heart . . . not that seven is perfect or that there are just seven and no more . . . I believe there are many more things. We are still just learning all that God has for us. Never close your mind to what is on His heart.

"We teach world vision on the basis of the whole Bible, on the basis of the last words of Jesus Christ and on the basis of Acts 1:8. The Great Commission is to get the gospel to every creature.

"Have you ever caught the idea that you are to have a world vision? God wants every one of us to have more than a casual interest in every nation of the world—to be concerned about what impact we can have. The Navigators are in many countries. Our goal is to serve in every major country of the world. We are not trying to start a new mission, but to go and give hands and feet and to serve the present groups that are already there or will be going there.

"These last three stars form the handle that acts as the fulcrum. This is how we reproduce reproducers.

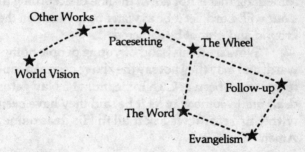

"It all starts with the Christ-centered, Spirit-filled life. . . . That's the beginning of production. Then we go into the Word of God and out into evangelism and follow-up. . . . That's reproduction. Not just one fruit tree for God's glory, but producing the seed from which will come many fruit trees which will reproduce orchards around the world, for His glory. Nothing less will do!

"I trust I haven't been preaching at you, but I have wanted just to talk with you and share with you what has been on my heart since that night on the roof of the Paris hotel. Now I want you to follow with me as I pray:

"'Lord, if anything has been said which is from You which You want to impart to these hearts, do cause it to remain and become a part of their lives. We do look to the Holy Spirit to put His seal on what is from You. And, Lord, if tonight I have done like I do so many times, gotten off the beaten path or said something that is not down the line or according to Your will, Lord, let it be as water poured out on the ground and cannot be gathered.

"'Now send this band of young people homeward, and may they not say they have been at a conference, nor been at Glen Eyrie, nor at a Navigator deal, but in some way let it be said they have been with Christ, and we ask it all in His dear name, Amen.' That's it!"

Source Notes

Chapter 2, page 14
Oswald J. Smith, *The Man God Uses* (London: Marshall, Morgan & Scott, 1953), pages 8-9.

Chapter 3, page 33
E.M. Bounds, *Power Through Prayer* (London: Marshall, Morgan & Scott, n.d.), pages 9-10.

Chapter 4, page 50
John Milton Gregory, *The Seven Laws of Teaching* (Grand Rapids, Mich.: Baker Book House, 1954), page 6.

Chapter 5, page 60
Oswald J. Smith, *The Man God Uses*, page 12.

Chapter 5, page 67
Betty Lee Skinner, *Daws: The Story of Dawson Trotman, Founder of The Navigators* (Grand Rapids, Mich.: Zondervan, 1974), page 40.

Chapter 8, page 112
LeRoy Eims, *The Lost Art of Disciple Making* (Grand Rapids, Mich.: Zondervan; Colorado Springs: NavPress, 1981), page 83.

Chapter 9, pages 159-160
Field-Marshal Montgomery, *The Memoirs of Field-Marshal Montgomery* (Cleveland, Ohio: The World Publishing Co., 1958), pages 76-77.

Chapter 12, page 200
The "Big Dipper" is a grouping of seven stars within the northern constellation called Ursa Major, or Great Bear. Together, the seven stars form an arrangement that resembles a ladle. The two stars on the end of the cup are called "pointers," because they line up with the North Star. In England, the Big Dipper is called "the wagon" or "the wain."